# DR. DAVID REUBEN'S

# ✚MENTAL✚
# FIRST–AID
# MANUAL*

W9-AWE-188

**\*INSTANT RELIEF FROM TWENTY-FIVE
OF LIFE'S WORST PROBLEMS**

PINNACLE BOOKS          NEW YORK

DR. DAVID REUBEN'S MENTAL FIRST-AID MANUAL

A Pinnacle Books edition, published by special arrangement with Macmillan Publishing Co.

Macmillan edition published in 1982
Pinnacle edition / January 1985

ISBN: 0-523-42242-3

Can. ISBN: 0-523-43234-8

*Printed in the United States of America*

PINNACLE BOOKS, INC.
1430 Broadway
New York, New York 10018

9 8 7 6 5 4 3 2 1

# WHEN YOUR MIND IS WORKING OVERTIME—
# MAKE IT WORK FOR *YOU*!

### Anxiety

At one time or another, it will strike 100 percent of the population. The first step in permanently removing anxiety from your life is to understand exactly what anxiety is.

### Boredom

In French they spell it *ennui*. In any language it spells t-r-o-u-b-l-e. Dr. Reuben shows you how to kick the mental opium habit.

### Burnout

The truth is that you don't *really* burn out, you burn yourself free! When you look at it that way, burning out is the best thing that ever happened to you!

### Depression

Your fate and your future life are not determined by your temporary feelings of desperation. *You have the power to say, "I simply refuse to be depressed!"* It works.

### Orgasm

Female orgasm is like the weather. Everybody talks about it, but hardly anybody does anything about it. You *can't* do anything about the weather, but a woman *can* do plenty about achieving an orgasm.

*To my wife, Barbara,*
*whose love is the spring*
*from which all my inspiration flows*

# Contents

# Acknowledgments

Books don't write themselves. I put these words on paper, but it was my wife, Barbara, who really made it all possible. As always, she provided the atmosphere of love and tranquillity which is so necessary for anything worthwhile to happen.

David Jr. worked hard as copy editor, computer programmer, and production manager. Cathy and Amy managed the telephone calls and worked hard at keeping their daddy happy. Giselle provided smiles and kisses in abundance. David Tigran came along just in time.

A special thanks is in order for Scott Meredith, a gentlemen, a scholar, and a truly literate man. Scott is the kind of friend every author should have. Jack Scovil also helped when he was needed most.

George Walsh, my editor and friend, knows his craft as few others do. It has always been a pleasure to work with him.

Finally, I want to thank the thousands and thousands of readers all over the world who asked for this book and who, I hope, will enjoy it.

# An Open Letter to My Readers

Dear Friends:

In response to thousands of letters from all around the world, I am happy to be able to deliver this book to you. As I was writing every word of it, I kept your question in mind: "In this strange and violent world that we live in, how does a person find happiness?" I am confident that this book will unlock the door to your personal happiness—just as you asked.

Obviously in a single book it was impossible to cover *every* one of life's worst problems. I tried to pick the ones that were the most dangerous, the most troubling, and the most frequent in this crazy world of ours. I have a strange feeling that this book is going to be the first in a series. With that in mind, if you have a particular problem that you would like covered in the *next* book, I'd be delighted to hear from you. You can write me at the following address:

Dr. David Reuben
c/o Scott Meredith
845 Third Avenue
New York, New York 10022

I'm also very interested to hear about your experiences in applying the principles of this book to *your* life. Please write me about them. I can't promise to answer every letter, but I solemnly promise to *read* every letter personally. I'd like to hear from you.

With warmest personal wishes for your happiness,

DR. DAVID REUBEN
*New York City*

# Dr. David Reuben's Mental First-Aid Manual*

## *Instant Relief from Twenty-five of Life's Worst Problems

# 1
# Mental First Aid

THE NAME OF THIS BOOK is *Dr. David Reuben's Mental First-Aid Manual*—and that's what it's all about. It is the complete manual of emotional first aid for life's worst problems—the first book specifically designed to provide immediate help for the overwhelming tension, anxiety, and depression produced by acute emotional crises.

There has never been a book like this before—and yet today, the need is geater than ever. In our tumultuous almost chaotic modern society, most of us undergo more emotional stress in a month than our parents experienced in a year. Today it is a rare individual who has not had to cope with divorce, drugs, unemployment, alcoholism, or depression—either personally or with somebody close to him. Almost without exception people with these problems suffer intensely and unnecessarily simply because they don't know how to deal aggressively with the fundamental problems. And there has been no way for them to learn— until now.

Let's take a practical example. If tomorrow morning at nine o'clock your world comes crashing down, what do you do? Where do you turn? Up until now these have been the only alternatives:

1

1. Psychiatry: A long, expensive, and still controversial approach. Psychiatry is *least* effective in relieving acute, excruciating emotional pain. It requires months if not years to produce its benefits, and its cost is truly out of the reach of the people who need it most.

2. Drugs: It is painfully obvious to almost everyone that drugs such as tranquilizers and antidepressants don't *solve* emotional problems. Almost invariably they actually block the solution of the current crisis by impairing the individual's ability to analyze his or her situation. The brittle euphoria produced by modern tranquilizers is the sufferer's worst enemy.

3. Religion: It is no secret that most Americans have lost confidence in organized religion as a source of emotional guidance. More and more each day they feel that religion is out of touch with the realities of everyday life, and they reject priests, ministers, and rabbis as dependable emotional guides in times of severe distress.

4. Traditional Self-Help Books: Unfortunately, nearly all of these tend to be stamped from the same mold. Superficially they vary only with the latest fad. For example, the recent spate of "self-assertion" and "intimidation" books produces a kind of synthetic arrogance, brittle and fleeting, which can occasionally *postpone* the inevitable; but when the emotional crash comes, it does twice the damage. Another major category of "psychoanalyze yourself" books is the Pollyanna group. Think good thoughts, always be optimistic, and nothing can affect you. With the first emotional crisis, most followers of these books are reduced to quivering jelly.

5. Exotic Solutions: These are a kind of catchall, including things like high intensity seminars offered by ex-saxophone players, transplanted Eastern pseudo religions, and other thinly disguised business propositions. They usually represent acts of desperation and have little application or appeal for the average person.

Most important of all, none of these even questionably

effective solutions are available when you need them most. If you have an accident at home, you can pluck a first-aid manual off your book shelf, flip the pages to the appropriate section, and find the information that will enable you to deal quickly and effectively with the emergency situation. If you are the victim of one of life's many *emotional* accidents, there is no such book on your shelf.

*But there can be.* This *Mental First-Aid Manual* is designed to help you cope with emotional accidents. It provides—succinctly, authoritatively, and precisely—what you need to know to regain control, confidence, and serenity in the face of life's lowest blows. It's there twenty-four hours a day, seven days a week—available to help you when you need it *most*. Let's take a moment to look at a few sample situations in which *Instant Relief* might come in handy.

You arrive home from work at six o'clock, tired as usual. There's a strange car in your driveway—and a police car at the curb. With mounting apprehension, you walk into your living room. There you find a doctor you've never seen before injecting your wife with a sedative. There are two federal agents sitting on your couch. They tell you that your sixteen-year-old son has just been shot in a drug raid. What's the *first* thing you do? What's the *second* thing you do?

You've been with the same company for eighteen years—working your way up from salesman to senior vice-president. Three months ago your firm merged with a big international company and you were "merged" out of your job. This is your one hundred and eighty-first day of unemployment. You're sitting at your kitchen table adding up your expenses—$4,500 a month—and your income—$912 a month. You've sent out fifteen hundred résumés and made over a hundred personal visits—without a single job offer. Nobody seems to want a fifty-one-year-old ex-senior vice-president. If it keeps up like this for another month, you're going to lose your house and your car. Now you're desperate, and finally this morning you feel an unbearable depression beginning to descend on you. What do you do?

You're a woman, forty-three years old with three children, ages eleven, nine, and seven. It's eleven o'clock in the morning, and you're sitting in the living room with your children around you. They're all crying. Your husband had his first heart attack a year ago—and he just had his second one twenty minutes ago. This time he died. The first heart attack and the disability that went with it took all your savings. You haven't worked in twenty years, and you don't know who's going to take care of your kids. You feel like crying, too, but the tears won't come. What do you do?

You are a successful lawyer. You're forty years old, and you have everything life can offer—a comfortable house in a prestigious neighborhood, a good wife, fine kids, and plenty of money. Your income is well over $100,000 a year, you own ample real estate, and you have more clients than you can handle. You've always wanted to be a judge, and the opportunity is just around the corner. There's only one little problem. Suddenly nothing means anything to you anymore. Your family, your law practice, your friends—they all seem so shallow, so pointless, so empty. The judgeship that you've dreamed about since you were eleven years old now seems like a waste of time. For the past week you haven't even been able to make it to the office. Without any particular reason, more than once in the past few days you've thought of killing yourself. Today it seems the only solution to your problems. What do you do?

It's five thirty in the evening. You're just hanging up the telephone. The call was from your best girl friend. She says that she saw your husband go into a motel with his twenty-two-year-old blond secretary an hour ago. You've been married eleven years, and things haven't been going that well lately. You've suspected that your husband might be cheating on you for about six months, but this is the first real evidence you've had. He's due home in half an hour. What do you do?

What you *do* in each of these cases—and in dozens more just like them—is reach for your *Mental First-Aid Manual*. Cross-referenced and instantly available, you find precisely what you need to know immediately to stop the mental pain you feel. You find honest, believable, proven means of dealing with your acute reality problem—no matter what it is.

Ideas of suicide? Turn to the section on Suicide. The ways to promptly regain control are there—right before your eyes. Alcoholism? The only really effective way to deal with alcoholism is laid out in black and white before you. Anxiety? Drugs? Depression? Financial problems? Chronic illness? Feelings of hopelessness? Divorce? Problems with children? Help can be at your fingertips. Tried and tested emotional first aid is no farther away than your bookshelf. The worst problems that human beings ever have to face are faced in my *Mental First-Aid Manual*—directly, realistically and with confidence.

*Dr. David Reuben's Mental First-Aid Manual* is a book that everyone will want to read, to keep for themselves, and to give to those they care about the most.

# 2
## Your Secret Enemy

AS YOU READ THESE LINES there are two possibilities. Either you feel really bad—depressed, confused, angry—or you don't. If you don't feel bad, just wait a while and you will! What am I saying? Well, sorry to say, it's true. That's the fate of human beings. We feel fine; everything's going great until all of a sudden, when we least expect it—*bang!* Our life goes into a nose dive. So if you've turned to this section because you have a really serious problem to face, keep reading—you've come to the right place! On the other hand, if you're just glancing over these pages out of curiosity, you're *still* in the right place. There's no better time to prepare for problems than *before* they happen. So, hang on, here we go!

This entire book is simply a *Mental First-Aid Manual* for emotional accidents. We're not going to waste any time on complicated theories or far-out philosophy. What we're going to do is figure out what makes it *hurt* and then do what we have to do to take the hurt away. Let's get started with a simple and very painful experience: hitting your thumb with a hammer as you're driving a nail. Think about it carefully. There are actually *two* kinds of physical pain. The first one is acute and intense. It hurts a lot when you first zap that thumb. Then that pain disappears and is immediately followed by a less intense, long drawn-out ache—a dull throbbing that can last all night. Remember?

Okay. But there's another kind of pain attached to hitting yourself with a hammer that follows right in the footsteps of the physical pain. That's the mental suffering that goes along with it. As you stand there watching the hammer go straight for your poor little thumb, you can see it about to happen but it's too late to do anything about it. You stand there helplessly while you mash a tiny piece of your own body! Wow! Then when the hammer hits, you wince because you didn't have any way to prevent the blow. It's like, "Oh, *what* am I doing to myself?"

But that's not the worst part. The worst part is the *mental* suffering that goes along with the subsequent hours of throbbing. You keep saying to yourself, "Why did I do it? What happened? How could I be such a dummy?" It's no exaggeration to say that the pain of the mental throbbing is often worse than the painful physical throbbing. And here's a fascinating little clue: It doesn't matter if you're alone or in a group as far as the *physical* pain is concerned—it's exactly the same. But if there's even *one* witness to the tragedy, the mental suffering can be ten times worse.

Well, so far I haven't told you too many things you didn't know—but hang on, it's going to get very interesting very quickly now, like in the next word. That word is *"why"?* Oh, I can tell you why your thumb hurts—that's easy and *unimportant*. What we really have to know pretty quick is why your *mind* hurts—why your being aches, why a simple blow to your thumb can make you angry, depressed, even *violent*. Oh, you never throw the hammer on the floor or kick the dog or yell at the kids when you clobber your thumb? You never say "Look what you made me do?" What's that? Maybe once in a while? Okay. Let's keep moving.

The reason you feel so bad when you hurt yourself

physically is because at the precise moment you strike the blow, you set in motion a massive psychological aggression against yourself! You unleash a monster that perpetually lies half asleep deep within you just waiting for the chance to tear you to pieces. Think about it. As soon as you feel the hammer strike, you think, "You idiot! You can't even hammer a nail right!" That's the first attack of *you* against *you*. That one's the same for everybody. The next zinger depends on your individual case. If you're a professional secretary or typist, what follows instantly is something like: "All right, stupid, that's two days' pay down the drain when you need it the most!"

If you're a father, the second zinger may be: "Making a fool of yourself again in front of your kids, Daddy?"

If you're a housewife, it could be: "See, you even have to do the carpentry around here!"

All these accusations have one thing in *common*—and that's what's going to help us as much as anything else to make ourselves *immune* to so much of the emotional pain that blights every human life. That one thing in common is the fact that all these accusations *come out of the same mold*. They are like broken records. *Everyone* in the world—a Pygmy, an Eskimo, a stockbroker in Paris, a cabdriver in Tokyo, a poor farmer in Brazil, and you— suffers exactly the same way under the same circumstances. Nobody feels good when they hurt themselves. Nobody breaks out in a grin when their child is sick. Nobody feels happy when they're down to their last dollar or franc or yen. And the inner insults that come pouring down on their heads—from their own personal monster—all say *exactly* the same thing.

But hang on a minute. I can hear you saying it now. I'm supposed to help you overcome the acute pain of specific lifetime tragedies. What's all this about hammering your thumb and some Inner Monster? How about dealing just with the specific problem? Well, that's an excellent idea—if you want to keep suffering. The whole concept that makes

*Dr. David Reuben's Mental First-Aid Manual* so different and so effective is that by understanding the *one* basic problem that produces emotional pain, you can apply it to each of its dozens of individual variations. And every emotionally painful experience you will ever have will be only a rerun of the typical emotional accident we're working over now. Okay? Let's continue.

It's time for a little summarizing. As soon as something bad happens to you—physical or mental—your Inner Monster gets off a volley of shots at your head. He works in exactly this fashion:

The first attack accuses you of being stupid. He says in effect: *What has just happened is your own fault! You're stupid and that's why it happened!*

The next attack, which follows in miniseconds, says something like: *This isn't the first time you've done it! You've always been a dummy!*

If there are witnesses, the third wave of hate from your Inner Monster goes like this: *Not only are you a loser but everyone knows it! Here are the witnesses that will gladly confirm what I've been telling you all these years!*

Now does it begin to fall into place? That's why if you whack your thumb and your husband or wife is present and says, ''Gee, you're always doing that!'' it drives you right out of your mind. Their innocent (maybe) observation simply confirms exactly what you're hearing from inside your head. You feel like hitting *them* with the hammer? I don't blame you.

So that's the central core of emotional suffering in human beings. You have a bad experience in reality—that funny little world in which we all have to live. Whatever goes wrong in your daily life is then suddenly magnified ten times, a thousand times, a million times—by your own Inner Monster—to make it seem *overwhelming*. Then you suffer . . . and suffer . . . and suffer. Your mind piles imaginary disaster upon imaginary disaster, and the final result is unbearable guilt or depression or anxiety—or all three.

Now let's take an example. It happened to Sally, although in one form or another it's happened to everybody. Let her tell it:

"I don't know why it upsets me so much, Doctor. It was really unimportant."

Sally paused for a moment and brushed her long reddish hair away from her cute little baby face. She wrinkled her brow: "Well, maybe it was more important than I thought. Anyhow, this is what happened. I had a date last Saturday with Ken—we've been going together on and off for about six months now and we're pretty close."

Sally's face flushed.

"At least I *thought* we were close! Anyhow, it was going to be one of those great parties—you know, good food, interesting people, a super house in the Hollywood Hills with a hot tub and a sensational swimming pool. I had this new outfit I'd just spent two hundred and ninety dollars on and . . . and . . . Ken never showed up!"

"He never showed up?"

Sally was biting her pretty little lip now—hard.

"That's right. He never showed up! At nine o'clock—half an hour after he was supposed to arrive—he called. It was really bad. He mumbled something about having a bad cold and would I please understand. Would I please understand? *Understand?* Understand *what?*"

The tears were rolling down Sally's pretty cheeks now.

"Why are you so upset?"

She answered through clenched teeth: "*Upset? Upset!* What makes you think I was upset, Doctor? Two hundred and ninety dollars down the drain, my roommate sitting in front of me dying of laughter, and I *knew* that he was going to the party with someone else! As a matter of fact, the next day I called a friend of mine who had been at the party and she confirmed it. There's nothing upsetting about *that*, is there, Doctor?''

"Of course you're right, Sally. It was plenty upsetting—and now let's see exactly *why*."

What Sally went through was the familiar *Big Three:*

1. When Ken didn't show up—and finally called and canceled the date—her Inner Monster let fly: *It's your own fault!*

That message can take many forms: *If only you had been prettier, if only you had been sexier, if only you had been smarter, if only you had been richer, et cetera, et cetera.*

In Sally's case it turned out that the accusation was *if only you had been sexier.* That was enough to make her suffer plenty.

The next blow came on schedule—immediately.

2. *This isn't the first time!*

Well, big deal! Unfortunately, Sally's defenses were weakened from the first attack and she was vulnerable. Her little monster began confronting her with all the times she'd been rejected by the opposite sex: *Remember Chuck? You thought you were going to get married to him. What a dummy you were! And then there was Bill—you didn't last a month with him! Oh yes, let's not forget Carl—that was going to be the perfect match. Isn't that what you told all your friends?*—and on and on and on.

It doesn't matter that Sally wasn't to blame for any of these minor mishaps—she got clobbered with them right then and there.

Then on to the grand finale, number three! Her roommate, who wasn't overly considerate (and has since been replaced), started to giggle when she saw the turmoil reflected on Sally's face. That immediately led to shock number three:

3. *Not only are you a loser but everybody knows it! See, here's your own roommate to confirm it!* Sally's slightly

hateful roommate pulled the emotional roof down on Sally's head.

Okay. We're going to provide instant relief for twenty-five of life's worst personal catastrophes, and we're going to see that the suffering produced by each emotional disaster follows more or less the same pattern as we've seen in the case of Sally. That's actually very good news because if every individual emotional problem was completely different it would be like typing on a Chinese typewriter with five thousand different characters. Just learning the patterns would take all our time—leaving nothing for attacking the problem.

But before we move on to specifics, let's pause just a moment to look at a couple of tiny—and tremendously important—details of Sally's broken date. Understanding them is going to be extremely important later on. First, the pain that Sally felt was all out of proportion to the real damage she suffered. What's one Saturday night more or less in the lifetime of a pretty girl? But that's a characteristic pattern in the panorama of emotional disasters—*the pain is all out of proportion to the actual loss*. Sometimes the pressure is applied in reverse. A person can *temporarily* feel much less pain than seems to be appropriate in a given situation. Some obvious examples that we'll get to before we finish are serious illness and unemployment.

The second important and very subtle detail of Sally's broken date was that she suffered almost as much in the retelling *three months later* as she did the night it happened! There were tears, frowns, drops of sweat on her upper lip, clenched fists—all inappropriate ninety days after being stood up. But that's a typical and deadly characteristic of the human mind under emotional stress. The Inner Monster never lets you forget! You are forced to relive over and over and over again the same suffering and humiliation a year later as if it were yesterday. Did you ever hear someone say, "I can't get it out of my mind"? Did you ever say it yourself? You did? Well, that's what we're talking about.

Let's keep these two tiny and vital details in mind as we continue to progress toward the goal of *Dr. David Reuben's Mental First-Aid Manual*. On to Chapter Three!

# 3
# The Problem Within the Problem

THIS VERY MOMENT is a critical moment in your life. Before you finish reading this chapter, *if you want to,* you will have the means of avoiding most of the pain and suffering that affect human beings. Too good to be true? Keep reading!

It was cool in my office, but the beads of sweat stood on Craig's upper lip.

"I just don't know what's going to happen to me, Doctor. I just don't know! I'm going out of my mind!"

Craig was about thirty-five. He wore a charcoal gray suede sport jacket, a pale blue shirt open at the neck, and sunglasses.

"What do you mean, Craig? What's the problem?"

He rubbed the back of his neck.

"You mean what *isn't* the problem, Doctor! I don't even know where to start!"

"How about the beginning?"

A faint smile formed on his lips.

"Okay, I might as well. Here's the story. About a week ago my life started falling apart. I'm the assistant manager

14

of a big restaurant here in town, and last week I sent my career into a nose dive. I still can't believe it!''

Craig squirmed uncomfortably.

"First, I have to tell you it was a great job. This place is part of a national chain, and I was on my way up to manager and then maybe in a few years to vice-president. It was going to be a geat future—and now it's all gone!''

Suddenly Craig slapped himself on the forehead with the palm of his hand.

"Was I an idiot! All for nothing!''

"Hey, Craig, how about letting *me* in on this?''

"Okay, Doctor, here it is. I was on duty about two weeks ago on the late shift—we don't close until three a.m. on Saturdays. This fat guy came in with a girl—obviously underage. We have—I mean *they* have—a bar, and so you have to be careful to keep minors out. In this town the cops'll close you down in a minute for that. The fat guy obviously had a couple of drinks in him, and the girl was a little out of it too. I don't know whether it was pills or what. Anyhow, Gladys, the hostess, seated them, but then she came over and told me about it. I went over and introduced myself and asked politely if I could see the girl's I.D. You know, a driver's license or something. We have—I mean, we *had*—a regulation way of saying it. What I was supposed to say was: 'I'm sorry, Ma'am. This has nothing to do with you, but the liquor law requires us to ask for identification from anyone who looks youthful. If you don't mind, could you please show me a driver's license or something?' I mean, what could be more polite than that?''

"It sounds pretty good to me, Craig. Go on.''

"Well, it wasn't so good. She looks at the fat guy like I'm crazy, and I can see he's getting mad. He grabs me by the arm—hard. I didn't like that too much, but I know how to treat customers. I just took it easy.

"He said, 'Listen, Buddy-Boy, if you don't want trouble just bug off!'

"I kept cool. I just said, 'I'm sorry sir, but I don't have any choice in the matter. The liquor laws say I have to ask for identification.' Then it happened."

"What happened?"

"He jumped up and gave me a shove."

"What did you do?"

"I picked up his napkin and dropped it on the floor."

"You dropped his napkin on the floor? Wasn't that a strange thing to do?"

Craig laughed long and hard.

"I can see, Doctor, you've never been in the restaurant business. Look, when I have to do something like that I always alert our security guys. Before we got to be a big corporation we used to call them bouncers. We run a three hundred-seat restaurant and a fifty-stool bar. We always have at least three big fellows on the premises, just in case. Well, when I drop a napkin it's a sign I want some help. Nothing serious. If it's big trouble, we drop a glass on the floor. Anyhow, Bennie and Steve suddenly appeared. Together they weigh about five hundred and sixty pounds, and if you stack one on top of the other, they're twelve and a half feet tall."

"Impressive."

"That's the idea. Anyhow, I asked again for the I.D., but the fat guy saw Bennie and Steve and he started to leave. He asked Gladys my name on the way out. She had to tell him—I don't hold that against her. That was it!"

"What do you mean, 'That was it'?"

"That was it. Monday when I showed up for work they told me I was terminated. It seems that the fat guy was our meat supplier. He called the president of our company at home on Sunday and told him I 'insulted' him. That was it. Now I'm in for it!"

"In for it? How?"

Craig put both hands to his head.

"No job, no recommendations, no unemployment. And all for being an idiot. If only I hadn't done it that way. I could have just ignored it. I'd still have a job and a future. That company is so big that I'll never get a job in the restaurant business in my life! And that's not all!''

''That's not all? What else?''

''Well, when I got fired like that I was really mad. I went down the street and I had a few beers to let off steam. Then on the way home I scraped somebody's fender and the police showed up. Now they have me for drunken driving. I wasn't really drunk, but it's a four hundred dollar fine for the first offense and I don't have the money. Oh, it gets worse and worse. I was so upset I had a fight with my wife and now she's not even talking to me. I haven't had a decent night's sleep in two weeks and I can't even think straight. What an idiot I turned out to be!''

Craig's unfortunate experience is a perfect example of the way the Inner Monster works on every human being. Notice that he suffered the same way as Sally. *The pain he felt was all out of proportion to the damage he had suffered*. After all, it was only a job that he'd lost—not an arm or a leg or a member of his family. In addition, the pain persisted far beyond the original experience. Weeks after the episode he was suffering as much or more than he had the night of the occurrence.

What should Craig have done differently to avoid the pain and suffering and loss that he exposed himself to? As soon as he got fired his Inner Monster started accusing him like never before. Let's take those accusations one by one and analyze them:

1. *It's all your fault!* The easiest way to defuse this accusation—strange as it may seem—is to *admit it!* Let Craig say to his Inner Monster: ''Okay, it's my fault. I don't deny it. Maybe I should have called the manager at home and passed the buck to him. But I take all the blame.''

What happens if you do that? It seems as if you'd taken instant mental aspirin. Suddenly you feel as if a tremendous load has been lifted from your shoulders. The accusation *"It's all your fault!"* suddenly dries up. And the truth is it *was* your fault. Just like hitting your finger with the hammer—*you did it*. But so what? The problem isn't *who did it*. The problem is *what to do about it*.

2. *This isn't the first time you've done this!* Of course it isn't the first time you've had a problem that you had to solve. Unless you're one day old you've had a lifetime of problems. It's also true that you've brought on a lot of these problems yourself. So what else is new?

The point is that you must not fall into the trap—that almost everyone falls into—of arguing with your Inner Monster about *who's to blame for the situation*. That kind of arguing leads you nowhere and only diverts you from your real goal: *solving the problems!*

By the way, isn't it fascinating to observe that arguments between people follow exactly the same pattern as the arguments between you and your *Inner Monster*? When something goes wrong notice how often a husband or a wife or a boss or a teacher or a co-worker launches an attack based on "It's all your fault!" followed by "This isn't the first time you've done this!" Your Inner Monster only sets the pattern for the *Outer* Monsters to follow. All the people around you have their own Inner Monster working inside them, constantly accusing them and attacking them. It shouldn't be a surprise that they follow the only pattern of attack and accusation they know—the one that has been used against them right from the beginning. Once you understand *that,* your life becomes much simpler. You can anticipate what kinds of attacks you are going to experience from the people around when something goes wrong. More important, you know exactly how to deal with them.

3. *Everybody knows what a dummy you are!* This particular accusation has real force only if you have tried to deny accusations *one* or *two* above. These are all general accusations that can be used against any human being anytime. Remember the famous story about the practical

joker who picked six prominent and wealthy men in his city at random? One night for no reason at all he sent them all the same telegram: "FLEE AT ONCE! INVESTIGATION BEGINS TOMORROW!"

At 8:00 a.m. the next they were all at the airport taking the first flight out.

Everyone is vulnerable to the dual accusation that they are foolish *and* that everyone knows it. So what? Keep constantly in mind the fact that life is *not* a popularity contest. Your worth as a human being does *not* depend on how many people like you. It depends on what you do with your life and what kind of person you are. If everyone in the world were to love you and you had twenty-five cents, you could buy a cup of coffee.

But there's something else. The third accusation of the Inner Monster is the most dangerous of all because of the damage it can cause you. You can defuse the first two accusations by admitting them—after all they are usually true. Besides, you don't lose anything by pleading guilty to them *provided* you go on to take the steps that we'll discuss in the next few pages. But the third accusation is different.

The Inner Monster can call you stupid and clumsy and inept all day without affecting you very much until one tiny event occurs. Once that event and the accusation coincide, you're in for it! Let's see exactly how it works.

It's 6:00 p.m. on a Thursday. Ted is just getting home. He walks in the door.

TED: Hi, Honey! I'm home.
SANDY: (Calls weakly from kitchen) I'm in here, Ted! In the kitchen!
(Ted throws his jacket on the sofa and goes into kitchen. The cabinets are all open, pots and pans cover the counter tops, a roast sits in a big pan on top of the stove. It is burned to a crisp. His daughter,

Kim, four years old, sits on the counter top by the sink. Her left knee is bandaged, and there are scratches on her face.)

TED: What the devil is going on here! What happened?

SANDY: (Wipes a smudge off her face with a dish towel, forces a tiny smile.) We've had a bad day, Ted. First, Caruso, the canary, got loose. Kim and I ran all over the house trying to catch him. During the chase Kim slipped and knocked over the lamp in the hall—the one your mother gave us. She cut her knee pretty bad. I got all upset and I couldn't get you at the office, so I tried to start the car but I couldn't find the keys. I took a cab to the doctor, and he fixed up Kim's knee. But I went out in such a hurry that I forgot to take the roast out and it got kind of cremated!

TED: (Getting mad) How much did all that cost?

SANDY: Well, the lamp . . .

TED: That was priceless!

SANDY: (Fighting back the tears) The cab was seven dollars each way—that's fourteen dollars. The doctor was forty-three dollars. I guess that's fifty-seven dollars. Then the roast was thirteen dollars. That's seventy dollars. Oh, Ted, I feel so stupid! (Bursts into tears)

TED: You are stupid! How many times have I told you to be more careful! If it wasn't for that dumb bird of yours, I wouldn't be out seventy dollars!

SANDY: (Throws dish towel on floor—hard) What? After all I went through to take care of *your* daughter all you care about is money! You spend seventy dollars on a pair of fancy golf shoes without giving it a thought! You are an insensitive clod!

TED: Me? Listen, when the least little thing happens you get so hysterical that you can't even start the car!

SANDY: (Methodically clears off the counter tops—throwing pots, pans, and roast on the floor—hard) Hysterical? I'm hysterical? I'll show you what hysterical is, you imbecile! (Little Kim begins to cry. It's going to be a long evening for everyone.)

What Ted and Sandy did—and what millions of husbands and wives are doing to each other every night—was *confirm* the third accusation of the Inner Monster. When all those little household catastrophes began piling up on Sandy, her Inner Monster said, as usual, "You're a dummy and everybody knows it!" Sandy was able to hold him off—more or less—by insisting that she *wasn't* dumb and acknowledging that her husband would testify against the Inner Monster on her behalf. That's the fascinating part. The Inner Monster works like a court of law. (More precisely, the courts of law work like Inner Monsters.) If you can get someone to testify that you are *not* guilty, that you are *not* dumb, the Inner Monster has to drop the charges. Sandy knew instinctively, and by experience, that as soon as Ted refuted the charges of the Inner Monster, she would suddenly feel better. But something went wrong. Ted not only didn't *refute* those charges, he *confirmed* them. That produced tremendous anxiety in Sandy and provoked a counterattack on her part. Unfortunately, that immediately confirmed the Inner Monster's accusations that were pending against Ted, and the result was what you saw.

Let's take a psychological X-ray of the conversation and see what actually happened:

TED: (Walks into kitchen) What the devil is going on here?

INNER MONSTER: *"See, Sandy, I told you everybody knew you were an idiot! Here's Ted, ready to testify for the prosecution!*

TED: (Getting mad) How much did all that cost?

INNER MONSTER: *Now you're going to get it, Sandy, dummy! Keep listening!*

TED: My mother's lamp! That was priceless!

INNER MONSTER: *Now get ready, Sandy! Here it comes! He's going to confirm everything I've been telling you for the past five hours! You'll love it!*

TED: You are stupid! How many times have I told you to be more careful! If it wasn't for that dumb bird of yours, I wouldn't be out seventy dollars!

INNER MONSTER: *Give it to her, Ted boy! She deserves it! Suffer, Sandy, suffer!*

So far Ted has taken the side of the Monster against Sandy. Now she's about to turn the tables on him. Watch how subtly it happens.

SANDY: (Throws dish towel on floor—hard) What? After all I went through to take care of *your* daughter all you care about is money! You spend seventy dollars on a pair of fancy golf shoes without giving it a thought! You are an insensitive clod!

INNER MONSTER: *Hear that, Teddy boy? That's what your mother said, that's what I've been telling you, and now here's the confirmation from someone who should know. You're a cheapskate and a clod! Now what do you say?*

Ted can't fight back against his Inner Monster since he doesn't even know that the Monster exists. So he takes aim at the only target in sight—the person who loves him most in the world, his wife, Sandy.

TED: Me? Listen, when the least little thing happens you get so hysterical that you can't even start the car!

Zing! Right in the bull's-eye! That hit Sandy hard! Listen to her Monster.

INNER MONSTER: *See! See! You Wouldn't believe me, but who knows you better than Ted? You're a clumsy hysterical little idiot! Now, suffer!*

Not too good. Every time Ted takes a whack at Sandy, Inner Monster takes two whacks at her. And then she takes a whack at Ted and Inner Monster doubles his punishment. She is about to clear the decks for action by dumping the burned roast and most of the kitchen equipment on the floor. She is escalating the hostilities, and there's no way to know where it will all end. If Ted and Sandy don't get their respective Inner Monsters under control, the last chapter of their personal tragedy will be written in the divorce court. What can they do? Let's rewind the tape and run it again as if Ted and Sandy knew what the Inner Monster was doing to them:

SANDY: (Calls weakly from kitchen) I'm in here Ted. In the kitchen!

TED: Wow! What happened? Are you all right, Honey? (Goes over and embraces Sandy)

SANDY: (Wilts in his arms) Oh, Ted, what a terrible day! Kim cut her knee, and I had to take her to the doctor, and everything went wrong!

TED: (Looking around) I can see. Well, that doesn't matter as long as Kim is all right. She's all right, isn't she?

SANDY: (Brightens momentarily) Sure! It was just a little gash.

TED: (Sees ashes of roast on stove) Say, why don't we all go out to dinner?

SANDY: (Sheepishly) Gee, I don't know. I'd like to, but between the doctor and the cab and all, I spent fifty-seven dollars and . . . and . . . (Looks up at Ted pathetically)

TED: (Swallows hard) So what! I'll get the fifty-seven dollars back from the insurance company. We can just go out for hamburgers, but I want to get you out of this disaster area. I can imagine what you've gone through today, Honey!

SANDY: (Hugs him around the neck, hard) Ted, I love you! I love you! (Kim smiles)

Did you notice two interesting things? Version Two didn't cost a penny more than Version One. It was just a different choice of words. (They were going to have to go out and have dinner anyway.) But the effect on their mutual happiness over the next eight hours—and the next eight years—is going to be very different. What Ted did in Version Two will pull them closer together. Version One will eventually destroy them.

The other interesting difference is that in Version Two, the Inner Monster couldn't get a word in edgewise. Ted unerringly blocked every possible accusation against Sandy. He absolved her of any of the blame, assumed responsibility for the expense himself, and rescued her from the scene of her humiliation. He also pointed out—correctly—that the welfare of their daughter was far more important than money. Another invisible bonus is the fact that he showed Sandy how *he* would like to be treated when the same kind of thing happens to him—tomorrow or the next day. Score one hundred points for Ted, one hundred points for Sandy, and one hundred points for their marriage. Score zero points for the Inner Monster.

Let's go back to Craig. He was a victim of the Big Three: *It's all your fault, this isn't the first time you've done this, and everybody knows what a dummy you are.* As soon as he got fired he reacted with indignation and resentment. He was aggressive, and he channeled his aggression into a few beers, some wild driving, and a traffic ticket. That made him even more tense and angry, and he tried to work off his tension by fighting with his wife. There's no doubt that being fired was a real threat. But his response was even more threatening to his own well-being. It was like a fellow who is walking down the street when a hold-up man sticks a gun in his ribs. The victim immediately responds by punching *himself* in the nose. That's what Craig did. And that's what he and I discussed on his first visit. About a week later, we talked again:

"You're looking better today, Craig."

"I'm feeling better, Doctor. I went to work on my problem the same day we discussed it. What a difference!"

"What do you mean?"

"Well, just doing something about it made me feel better. I did what you suggested. I went right to the president of the company and I talked to him. Wow! That fat guy was really a troublemaker!''

"How so?"

"Well, he told the president that I'd insulted him—that I threw him out and tore his jacket in the process. He really made it sound bad!''

Craig shook his head.

"What did you do?"

Craig smiled sheepishly.

"The wrong thing, of course. I got mad. I started to raise my voice, and then I remembered what you said. It was only the Inner Monster starting to give me the works. It helped. I calmed down right away. I just asked the president to call Gladys at home and ask her what happened. He did and she told him the truth. Then he called the fat guy right while I was there and told him to apologize to me or he could look for some other place to sell his meat. I was really impressed!''

"So am I."

"What do you mean, Doctor?"

"What I mean is that you proved just what I told you. You *can* fight back against your Inner Monster, and you can solve the problems that you never thought you could solve. You just proved it!''

Craig sighed deeply.

"Well, you were certainly right about that. Anyhow, my boss he put me on the phone and made the fat guy apologize to me. Now that he was sober he didn't seem to be such a bad guy. But I wasn't too impressed with that. He was bad enough to cost me my job. Anyhow, I'm back at work, and our president told me he liked the way I handled the whole matter. He's going to make me manager of the next restaurant where a vacancy comes up. Boy, that was a close call!''

"I'm not so sure, Craig. It was just an incident that could have happened any day of the week. What *was* a close call was the way you just let things happen to you without fighting back—without taking a stand. What about the drunken driving charge?''

Craig nodded.

''I almost forgot about that. I went to court and explained to the judge exactly what happened. He understood that it was just a kind of emotional weirdness. He continued the case for a year, and he said that if I didn't get into any more trouble, he'd dismiss it when it came up again.

''That's another example of what you can accomplish when you *make* things happen instead of let things happen.''

''Oh, that was just some more of my stupidity. It's all straightened out. You know, Doctor, there's one really important thing that I learned from all of this.''

''What's that, Craig?''

''Understanding how your mind works is the second hardest job in the world.''

''That's an interesting way to put it, Craig. Then what's the hardest job in the world?''

Craig smiled.

''Trying to get by *without* understanding how it works.''

Of course, Craig is right. In the pages that follow you can see how your mind works, and you can decide if you want to make it work for *you!*

# 4
# Alcohol

LET'S TEST YOUR KNOWLEDGE of alcohol and alcoholism. Answer the following five questions, true or false:

1. The secret to avoiding alcoholism is "learning how to drink."

2. Alcoholism is really a defect of metabolism—some people are just allergic to alcohol.

3. A shot of whiskey every day will help prevent heart attacks.

4. Drinking, in moderation, will help you live longer.

5. In itself, there is nothing harmful about alcohol.

Okay, time's up! If you marked any of these statements correct, give yourself a big fat *zero*. Or more precisely, give that big fat *zero* to all the newspaper articles and television programs that filled your head with all that silliness. In the paragaph that follows you will read something that you have never read before—the plain unvarnished truth about alcohol. What follows are scientific facts—with no moral judgment intended. Read the facts, then make up your own mind. Here goes.

The term "alcohol" refers to a family of organic chemicals which includes wood alcohol, rubbing alcohol, drinking alcohol, and dozens of other alcohols. The kind that people drink is called ethyl alcohol or ethanol. It is produced by the fermentation of natural sugars and contains two atoms of carbon, six atoms of hydrogen, and one atom of oxygen. It is clear liquid with a faint characteristic odor.

When you drink it, it directly affects several organs of the body, known as target organs. The organ that is most affected by alcohol is the brain. The effect of ethanol on the brain is progressive and increases with the dose. So far, so good. A few dry scientific details. Now it gets more interesting. The effect of drinking alcohol on the human brain is almost identical to the effect of ether or most other surgical anesthetics. The first stage, corresponding to a couple of drinks, is one of relaxation and euphoria. That's the first couple of whiffs of ether. A couple more drinks—or whiffs of ether—and the patient becomes excited and agitated. That's when the office manager starts telling off-color jokes in a loud voice at the company party. Another couple of drinks produce a stage of analgesia—literally "feeling no pain." That's when sexual inhibitions retreat and unwanted pregnancies advance. That's also the stage when the dentist can pull your tooth and you won't feel a thing. Keep drinking—or taking ether—and you reach the stage of muscular relaxation and incoordination. That's when you can't walk a straight line and start spilling your drink on your shirt front. Keep swallowing alcohol and you finally reach the stage of anesthesia. You don't feel a thing, you don't know where you are, and the doctor could saw off your leg without any complaint. About two hundred years ago, incidentally, that's exactly what doctors did. They poured whiskey down your throat until you conked out. Then they operated.

Another symptom of big doses of alcohol is amnesia. When you wake up the next morning, you can't remember anything. It can be embarrassing, for example, if you can't remember whom you got pregnant. It can be even more embarrassing if you can't remember who got *you* pregnant. You can summarize the effect of alcohol on the brain this way: It knocks out the various functions of the nervous system in a very precise pattern. First it affects thinking, then it affects feeling, then it affects judgment, then it affects physical control and coordination, and finally it affects consciousness. Carried to its ultimate extreme, it converts a human being into some kind of amoeba, collapsed in a heap with all the circuits turned off, barely existing.

From a purely scientific point of view it's obvious that the effect of alcohol on the brain is cumulative. That is, "drinking" alcohol is a toxic chemical, and it does the brain a tiny bit of damage with each exposure. Over a period of, say, twenty years of dedicated drinking, an individual ends up with chronic permanent brain damage. In some cases it may be mild. For example, an executive may begin to have trouble remembering names of his customers or an accountant can't do mental calculations quite the way he used to. In other cases, the damage is greater—a husband may become more irritable and withdrawn or a wife may lose interest in her personal appearance. Extreme examples end up with what doctors call Korsakoff's syndrome. This is an incurable mental illness that results from the physical damage that alcohol can do to the brain. Among the prominent symptoms are loss of recent memory, extreme lack of motivation, and a strange and inappropriate cheerfulness.

Alcohol also affects many other organs of the body. You must have seen those dumb articles saying a drink or two of whiskey a day is "good for your heart." Actually, it's quite the opposite. It has been proved conclusively that alcohol causes immediate *constriction* of the coronary arteries. So if you want your heart attack right away—no waiting—down a couple of drinks every night. The other fairy tale that always gets big play in the papers is the *amazing discovery* that drinkers live longer! Sure, and they can all walk on water and sing like canary birds. Whenever I read fairy tales like that I remember what they taught me in Statistics 101: "Figures don't lie but liars can figure." Ask yourself who did the studies and who paid for them. The answers should be very interesting. The undeniable truth is that alcohol is a toxic chemical which damages your mind and your body. It doesn't increase anybody's life expectancy—ever. You can prove it for yourself by checking the life expectancy of dedicated nondrinkers—Mormons, Seventh Day Adventists, and similar groups. That's when you'll really see how much even moderate drinking shortens your life.

And now let's get to the big question: Why do people drink? Well, there are two basic reasons. First, they drink because they are told to drink. Just for fun, one day count the number of times you are exposed to advertisements for alcoholic beverages—beer, wine, and liquor. If you don't count over one hundred advertising "impacts" (as they are known in the advertising business), you probably live in the Gobi Desert. And the people who tell you how wonderful it is to drink alcohol are very convincing. The ads use very sexy young ladies, handsome young men, impressive father figures, and everything else the liquor industry can think of. The settings are always plush and expensive, and the sell is very hard: *If you want to be happy, rich, and well liked, drink!*

Remember quite a few years back those whiskey ads featuring a "Man of Distinction"? An elegant and obviously wealthy gent dressed in a tuxedo standing in an oak-paneled library was shown nursing a glass of whiskey. The message was obvious. If you want to be rich and wear a tuxedo in your million dollar mansion, just drink their brand of whiskey. But what they never showed you was a drunk in filthy clothes, his red face covered with ugly scabs, lying on a urine-soaked mattress in a cheap flophouse. His mistake was switching brands, right?

The second reason for drinking is far more subtle. Drinking alcohol causes a temporary chemical lobotomy that human beings perform on themselves. Even the first drink hits hard at the most sophisticated part of the brain—the prefrontal lobes, right behind your forehead. This is where such heavy feelings as guilt, responsibility, loyalty, honesty, morality, fear and anxiety live. They are in fact soluble in alcohol. After a few drinks so many of the tensions and worries that come from these civilized values are washed away. That's why alcohol is the real sexual lubricant. That's why the more demanding and more difficult your job is, the more you welcome the "happy hour," when you can find relief in your favorite bar and wash away the tensions that float on the surface of your brain.

Incidentally, that's why they design bars—or cocktail lounges, if you prefer—the way they do. They are dark and soft and quiet—to enhance the effect of the drug alcohol on your brain. Just as opium dens are designed around the effect of opium on the brain—cots and quiet atmosphere—and places where people go to smoke mari-huana have nice colors and nice music, places where people imbibe alcohol are designed to get the best from the drug.

Now let's go to a trickier question. What is alcoholism? Who is an alcoholic? Like everything else, the medical "experts" have it all worked out. According to them a mild alcoholic is someone who is drunk four or more times a year. A moderate alcoholic is someone who is drunk more than twelve times a year or gets "happy" more than once a week. A severe alcoholic—well, you can imagine that for yourself! As with all rigid medical definitions, these don't make too much sense.

For practical purposes, an alcoholic is someone who drinks for the effect, who uses alcohol as a tranquilizing drug. That doesn't mean that an alcoholic has to be a falling-down drunk—it simply means that he or she uses drinking as a mental crutch. And that effect may vary from person to person. Sometimes a shy individual may take a few drinks to make it easier for him or her to relate to others. More than one salesman downs a few before calling on a difficult customer. Harried executives frequently unwind with a double scotch or two after a day in the corporate trenches. A few beers—and often many more than a few—greet the factory workers after the grueling assembly line grinds to a halt.

Are these people alcoholics? Sure they are. Not in the sense that they are deteriorated drunkards but in the sense that they use alcohol for its psychic effect—as a way of numbing their brains against the onslaught of the pressure and tension of their daily lives. Should they stop drinking? Ahh, that's another question and a very personal one. The advantages of alcohol have to be weighed carefully against the disadvantages. Let's list, to the best of our ability, the advantages of ethyl alcohol. Here they are:

1. Alcohol is a mild tranquilizer.

2. Alcohol is one of the two *socially acceptable* mind drugs. (Tobacco is the other.)

3. Alcohol is a *legal* mind drug.

4. In moderation, alcohol damages the body slowly and gradually.

Now let's look at the other side—the disadvantages of ethyl alcohol. Here they are:

1. Alcohol is expensive. A mild drinking habit can set you back at least 10 percent of your income. Drinking more alcohol or fancier brands can triple or quadruple that cost.

2. Alcohol causes loss of social control. Ninety percent of fatal auto accidents occur under the influence of alcohol. Eighty percent of all crimes of violence occur under the influence of alcohol. Seventy-five percent of suicides are related to drinking. More than half of all residential fires are linked with drinking.

3. Alcohol is an addicting drug—medically speaking. Sudden withdrawal produces a definite withdrawal syndrome. In mild drinkers, as in mild narcotic addicts, the symptoms of withdrawal are mild. In heavy drinkers the withdrawal

syndrome is very severe (including delirium tremens) and may end in death.

4. Alcohol can produce serious physical disease. Cirrhosis of the liver, chronic gastritis, kidney problems, obesity, neurological conditions, and other assorted diseases can be the end result of even moderate drinking over many years.

Now that all these facts are out in the open, the big question is, Should you continue drinking? That is, of course, your personal decision. But here are some factors to take into consideration:

1. *Don't be afraid to stop drinking.* The intense social pressure to drink and keep drinking should not be part of your decision—one way or the other. If, after you have weighed all the evidence, you decide you don't want to drink, it's your business and no one else's. The so-called friends you lose by not drinking were never real friends to begin with. You're lucky to be rid of them so easily. If they don't respect you for such an important decision, they're not worth the name "friend."

2. *Don't be intimidated by prodrinking propaganda.* We've all seen the articles gloating about what a failure Prohibition was in the United States. It's worthwhile looking into it because it can tell us a lot. Back in 1920 the United States prohibited the sale or consumption of alcohol. For thirteen years an immense country reduced its consumption of ethyl alcohol by about 90 percent. What happened? This is what happened.

*a*. In the thirteen years of restriction of alcohol, the death rate went *down* 18 percent!

*b*. As soon as drinking was legalized, in 1934, the death rate took a big jump upward. It increased a whopping *4 percent* in the first legal-drinking year alone! The death rate then continued to rise unrestrained until 1941 when antibiotics came into general use. That's when the death rate from infections fell 90 percent, easily masking the increased death rate related to alcohol.

*c*. After thirteen years of curtailed drinking, the divorce rate in the United States was at a historic low. As soon as liquor was legalized again, the divorce rate took off like a rocket and has never stopped since. Shall we drink to that?

If Prohibition was really so good, why was it repealed so suddenly? The answer to that is easy—and a tribute to the cynicism of politicians. In 1933 the United States found itself in the depths of an economic depression. One of the major financial contributors to the victory of the winning party was in the liquor business in a big way. Prohibition was costing him millions in profits. His candidate won, and drinking was legalized again. The excuse—to make the maneuver palatable to the average man—was that legalizing drinking would provide jobs! How about legalizing murder to provide work for grave diggers and undertakers?

So, if anybody tells you that Prohibition was a failure, you can tell them they're right—from a profit-making point of view. But from a human point of view, it was a sensational success.

3. *Don't be afraid to face reality*. I will never forget the words of my professor of pharmacology twenty-five long years ago when he observed that *a patient would be better off if he were addicted to heroin* (assuming he could get a reasonable supply at a reasonable price) *than if he were addicted to alcohol*. He went on to explain, correctly, that the heroin addict could continue working, would remain in good health (heroin does not produce brain damage or cirrhosis), and would be able to function well with his family. (Heroin addiction does not produce either the impotence or the paranoia of alcoholism.) He didn't recommend heroin addiction—*and neither do I*. Nor do I recommend the use of cocaine, marihuana, or methadone. But my professor pointed out—as I must—that all of those are much less harmful to the human mind and body than alcohol. They are all bad for you—don't use them—but alcohol does the most harm.

4. *The best way to stop is to stop—sometimes.* If you are a mild chronic drinker—two to four drinks a day—you can quit cold turkey. True, you will have a mild withdrawal syndrome, which may involve weakness, sweating, and an upset stomach. But you can take it, and it lasts only three days at the most. And once you are over it, you are over it.

If you are a heavier drinker, the risk of a bad withdrawal syndrome exists, although the risk is much less than the risk of continued drinking. Find a doctor who is experienced in treating and avoiding the alcoholic withdrawal syndrome and let him or her help you. Don't pick just any doctor because withdrawal from alcohol is a specialized problem. With competent medical help, you can get through it quickly and painlessly.

5. *Be honest with yourself.* You know—deep inside—if you have a drinking problem. Don't wait until you lose your job, mess up your marriage, kill someone on the highway, or any of the other thousand tragedies of alcoholism. Be absolutely honest with yourself, and make the decision that will be best for you—and for your family.

6. *If you need help, get it.* Getting out from under an addicting drug like alcohol is not always a do-it-yourself project. Sometimes a little bit of help from someone who knows what they are doing can go a long way. In general, there is no better group than Alcoholics Anonymous for that task. Yes, I know, they're not perfect but then who is? But at least they don't have any illusions about "learning how to drink" or "one little drinkee won't hurt me." Sometimes you may find a program for alcoholics where you work, through a trade union, or in the military service. *But get help if you need it. The life you save will be your own.*

You say drinking isn't your problem? You say it's the problem of your husband or your wife or your father or your mother or your son or your daughter? I'm sorry, but you're wrong. It's *your* problem. If someone you love is deep into alcohol, it is *your* problem. Don't be afraid to use the insight and the knowledge that you have now to help them—lovingly, compassionately, but with determination. When it's all over they'll thank you for it.

# 5
## Anxiety

IF SOMEONE ASKED YOU what single disease has inflicted the most suffering on the human race, what would you say? Cancer? Heart disease? Hardly. The one malady that has caused the most pain and suffering throughout the long history of mankind is none other than *anxiety*.

How come? Easy. First of all, cancer and the rest of the horrible diseases affect at most a small percentage of the population. Anxiety—at one time or another—strikes *100 percent* of the population of the world. There is no man, woman, or child on this planet who has not or does not suffer acutely from the razor-sharp pangs of anxiety. Second, there is no pill and there is no surgery that can cure this dreadful disease which has drained the happiness of so many billions. That doesn't mean that people haven't *tried* to find magical cures for this condition. The millions of gallons of alcohol in all forms that are consumed each week are desperate attempts to dissolve anxiety. The tons of tranquilizers that are gobbled so eagerly are part of the losing battle against anxiety. Drugs like marihuana, cocaine, heroin, and all the rest are hopeless attempts to control anxiety. The only problem is that none of this chemical warfare works. The pills, the booze, the drugs are all absorbed into the bodies and minds of billions of people each day, and the anxiety, if anything, gets worse.

So, nothing works? There's no hope? Fortunately, that's not true. *Almost* nothing works against this universal curse of mankind, but fortunately there is an effective way to eliminate anxiety from your life. If you're interested, just keep reading.

*The first step in permanently removing anxiety from your life is to understand exactly what anxiety is.*

That may not be as easy as it sounds. Listen to the way Nancy tells it:

"I know what you're going to tell me, Doctor! I don't want to hear it!"

I couldn't help smiling just a little.

"Okay, I won't tell it to you, Nancy."

Nancy looked disappointed.

"Okay, Nancy, what is it that you don't want me to tell you?"

Nancy lunged forward in her chair.

"Don't tell me to *stop fidgeting!*"

"Yes, I did notice that you were fidgeting a little bit."

*"I told you not to tell me to stop!"*

"But Nancy, I didn't tell you to stop. As a matter of fact, please keep fidgeting. It gives you something to do. And besides, you seem rather sensitive about it."

Nancy slumped back.

"Oh, Doctor, I just don't know what to do. I haven't slept in three nights. I'm worried sick."

"What's the problem, Nancy?"

"But that's just it, Doctor. There isn't any problem. I mean there are so many problems I just can't tell which one is bothering me the most. Actually, everything seems to bother me. Or the things that never used to bother me are starting to drive me crazy! You see, it doesn't make any sense! Oh, what am I going to do?"

The tears started rolling down Nancy's pretty cheeks.

"Well, the first thing to do might be to try and relax. Don't get me wrong—you can keep fidgeting if you want to, but try and relax while you're doing it."

Laughter came through the tears.

"Oh, Doctor, I'm so embarrassed about that! I didn't mean to make such a fuss when I first came in. Please forgive me—it's just part of the same problem. I get so sensitive about silly little things like that! Please forgive me."

"There's nothing to forgive you for—but you're forgiven. Now tell me, what are the three things that worry you the most?"

"Well, first there's my job. I'm an occupational therapist at a big hospital, and I'm afraid they're going to eliminate my job. They're cutting back on everything. Then there's Mike's mother. Mike's my husband, and his mother is talking about moving back to the town where we live. She won't live with us, but I don't even want her in the same town! And then there's the cost of living. We're barely making it now, and if prices go any higher, I don't know what we'll do!"

"You're worried about *that?*"

Nancy looked annoyed.

"What's wrong with that? Aren't those worries big enough!"

"Sure they're big enough—big enough to keep you from sleeping nights. But I think if we look at them carefully, we'll see that they're nothing more than 'pilot light' worries."

Her tone was incredulous.

" 'Pilot light worries?' What's that?"

"You know how gas appliances work, don't you? Like gas stoves and water heaters? There's a little tiny gas flame that burns all the time so that when the main burner gets switched on the gas ignites immediately and the heat goes way up. I know the pilot light is going out of fashion now that the cost of gas is up, but the comparison still holds.

"It's the same thing in your mind. You don't have any real worries right now so you have to invent a few little problems just to keep the flame of anxiety burning. That's your 'pilot light.' It keeps burning so that it's ready to ignite the main flame of anxiety at any time. There's not much you can do to keep them from eliminating your job at the hospital or to keep your mother-in-law from living in the town she wants to live in or to keep the cost of living from going up. But you let those things weigh on your mind just the same."

Nancy frowned.

"Hmmmm. That makes sense, Doctor. But why do I do it?"

"Because the vulture needs a place to land."

Nancy's mouth fell open.

*"What?"*

"It's the best way I know of illustrating it. The anxiety that you always have—the uneasiness and apprehension that is always with you—is like a big black vulture that constantly circles around your head. And like all big black birds, it needs a place to land. So it lands on feeble little branches like insecurity about your job, the threat of mother-in-law moving closer, or the worry that prices will go even higher. The point is you're anxious most of the time but you don't really know why. So you look for a place to hang your anxiety. You really had to think hard to come up with three big worries—that aren't really worries."

"Are you *sure* about that, Doctor?"

Now it was my turn to smile.

"Sure I'm sure, Nancy. If you want to test it, let's pretend we can wave a magic wand and make those three problems disappear. You have perfect job security, your mother-in-law is moving to Tahiti, and the prices are going to stay where they are for the next two years. Now how do you feel?"

Nancy squinted.

"I'm thinking."

A few moments went by. The corners of her mouth turned up slightly and her eyes twinkled.

"I see what you mean. As soon as I imagined those problems were out of the way, I started worrying about how much you were going to charge me and whether or not Mike was losing interest in me. You know, he's been just a tiny bit indifferent lately, and I wonder if it's my fault or . . ."

Nancy broke out into a broad smile.

"You're right! You're right! There I go again. What's behind all this craziness?"

"It's not really craziness, it's just the way human beings function. I like to call it the 'pecking order of problems.' "

"There you go again, Doctor. What do you mean by the 'pecking order of problems?' "

"I don't know if you've spent much time observing chickens, but they are exotic and mysterious animals. If you put a group of chickens together in the chicken yard— say twenty-five or so—they quickly organize themselves into a strange sort of society. One of them becomes the 'top' chicken and demonstrates it by pecking at chicken number two. Chicken number two never dares to peck back but immediately takes a peck at another chicken who becomes chicken number three. The process continues until it filters down to poor little chicken number twenty-five, who doesn't get to peck anybody at all."

Nancy perked up.

"I'm beginning to get the idea, but please go on."

"Sure. You—and everyone else—establish the same type of priority with your worries. Let's say you have a really bad disagreement with your husband and you are on the brink of separation. All your worrying capacity becomes concentrated on the awful prospect of seeing your marriage collapse. It weighs on you day and night, and you feel if only you can settle that problem, you will never worry about anything again. Have you ever had that experience?''

"Only about a thousand times, Doctor!"

"Then you know what I'm talking about. So when you finally make up with your husband, you feel a tremendous flood of relief that lasts . . . How long would you say it lasts, Nancy?''

Nancy thought a moment.

"With luck, I'd say about an hour."

"That's about average. Then problem number one pecks problem number two and the cycle starts all over again. Sometimes you get the flu or you crash the car a little or you get into a fight at work—and the anxiety level zooms upward again. The big black bird has found a place to land.''

"Whew! What a mess! How do I get out of it?"

"I agree it's a mess. The way to get out of it is to become aware of it. That's what happened to you just now. From now on you can be on your guard. Now you know that the anxiety you feel doesn't have *that* much to do with the specific problem that you may be facing at the moment.''

"I get that part fine, Doctor. But what do I do to avoid anxiety once and for all?''

"I'm not sure that you can completely get rid of anxiety in this crazy world we live in. They don't call this the 'Age of Anxiety' for nothing, Nancy. But there are some ways to get your anxiety under control so at least it doesn't cripple you the way it has been. One way might be to understand what *fear* is and how it's related to anxiety. Would you like to go into that?''

Nancy shrugged her shoulders.

"I've gone this far—I might as well go all the way!"

"Okay, hang on tight. About a million years ago when people lived in caves, it wasn't exactly the 'Age of Anxiety.' It was more like the 'Age of Fear.' When things happened they happened fast and violently. A saber-toothed tiger leaped out at you from behind a tree and growled. You got scared, the adrenaline starting pumping like never before, and you either shoved your spear into the tiger or ran like the dickens . . .''

Nancy interrupted.

"Or got eaten up?"

"I didn't want to dwell on that, but you're right—or got eaten up. In any event, the problem was solved within minutes. You got a good scare, you solved the problem—or the tiger solved it for you—and you calmed down. That was *fear*—intense, acute, and temporary. But as society evolved things got much more complicated and the fear gradually lasted longer and longer. When society became oriented around agriculture, the fear was 'Will the seeds grow?' or 'Will there be enough rain for the crops?' That stage was about midway between old-fashioned fear and modern anxiety. You worried but in short order your worries were resolved—one way or another. Either the seeds sprouted or they didn't. Either it rained or it didn't. It was just like making a parachute jump—you don't know exactly how it's going to end but you're sure that you're not going to be hung up there indefinitely."

"But nowadays things are different?"

"You bet they are! In this incredibly complex society there are dozens of problems that everyone has that just can't be resolved. They don't cause the same acute fear as the saber-toothed tiger or the semiacute fear as to whether the seeds will sprout or not. But they do produce a low-grade nagging uneasiness and insecurity that comes through as chronic anxiety that never goes away."

Nancy nodded her head.

"That big bird again?"

"Right. Only these days the problems seem impossible. The whole world has become so complicated. Just look at some of the sources of anxiety: Will your marriage last? Where do you really fit in the framework of society? Is there going to be a nuclear war? Do your friends really like you? Is there any future in your job? Is your life worthwhile? Are you going to get cancer? Why is everything so boring? And on and on and on.''

"That sounds like the average person has a whole squadron of big black birds doing power dives around his head!''

"You're pretty close to the truth, Nancy. Okay, what's the way out? As far as I know, there are only two effective solutions to the problem of anxiety. They are *mental activity* and *physical activity*. Mental activity means listing all the problems that bother you at any given time and dealing with them so that they don't bother you anymore.''

Nancy brightened up.

"I get it! Like the saying that they print on those little ceramic tiles for the kitchen: 'Please help me to change the things that I can change and to accept the things that I can't change, and please help me to tell the difference.' Is that it?''

"That's *almost* it, but not quite. The flaw in that little saying is that you can change a lot more things in this world than you think you can. A lot of the things that you think you have to accept, or that people tell you have to be accepted, are really within your power to change. But that's another story. Anyhow, after you make your list of the problems that worry you the most, write down what you can do about them—*and do it*. The secret is to take *some* kind of action about every problem, no matter how insignificant that action may seem. The reason it's so important is that action is just the first concrete step in solving the problem. You'll be amazed at how much better it will make you feel.''

"I'll try it, Doctor. I'll try anything.''

"You won't be disappointed. The other half of the solution to anxiety is *physical activity*. It's no secret that chronic anxiety produces muscular tension, headaches, arrhythmias of the heart, peptic ulcers, and a lot of other bad physical reactions. At the same time you attack your anxiety *mentally*, you can attack it physically with physical exercise. It doesn't have to be anything more strenuous than a good long walk, although swimming, running, tennis, bicycling, and whatever else you can manage are just as good. If every day you launch that kind of double-pronged attack against your anxiety, you'll be amazed and delighted at how well you feel.''

Nancy had an impish look on her face.

"You mean I'll actually be able to shoot down that big black vulture once and for all, Doctor?''

"Shoot him down, Nancy? I'm not so sure about that. But at least you might be able to trade him in on a little yellow canary.''

# 6
## Arrest

NOT SO LONG AGO, it was only dangerous criminals who were arrested. Burglars, bank robbers, and other assorted hoodlums were the only types who saw the inside of a police station. But nowadays things have changed. Obviously, you're a law-abiding citizen, but there are always cases of mistaken identity, auto accidents, income-tax problems and the like that can put you into direct and hazardous contact with various and assorted police agencies. While that kind of experience can never be what you'd call fun, if you know the ropes, it can be *relatively* painless. If you don't understand the legal procedures, it can be a miniature nightmare. Let Ron tell what happened to him.

Ron had a bushy black beard and carried his 225 pounds evenly distributed on his six foot frame. His style of dress could best be described as "Texas casual"—worn cowboy boots, superfaded Levi's, and an old army shirt from some long-forgotten war. His long curly hair hung down to his shoulders. When he spoke his voice was deep and resonant:

"I'm a professor of psychology at the junior college, Doctor, and what I learned about psychology last month, you won't find in any textbook."

Ron smiled grimly and shifted in his seat.

"Except maybe one they'd never publish. Anyhow, I was in my office at the college just about four weeks ago trying to decide where to eat lunch when my secretary told me there were two men from the district attorney's office waiting to see me. I was curious and I told her to send them in. If I'd only known what was going to happen, I would have gone out my office window right into the parking lot and headed straight for Mexico.

"Anyhow, they were two young guys in dark suits. They strolled in; one closed the door and stood in front of it while the other showed his badge and asked me what my name was. I told him. He started to ask me a whole bunch of questions, like who were my friends, where did I go on weekends, had I been outside the country lately, and a lot of weird stuff. I guess I got a little annoyed and told him to buzz off. Then he announced that he was conducting a narcotics investigation and I had better cooperate if I knew what was good for me! Man, I saw red! The *last* thing in the world I'm into is narcotics. No one is more against that than me. I told them they had the wrong address and I got up to go to lunch. I brushed the one in front of the door out of the way and rushed out. Wow! What a mistake!"

Ron winced as if it were happening all over again in my office.

"They had two gorillas waiting in the outer office, and they pounced on me like I was a ripe banana. In about two seconds I was handcuffed—tight—and tucked in the back of their police car. It was down to the station and into a hot little room where they spent the next four hours asking me stupid questions. And I must say, I gave all the wrong answers."

"What do you mean by 'wrong answers,' Ron?"

"Well, first I tried to be silly. They asked me why I had visited Jamaica, and I told them I went there to learn to pick coconuts. That kind of made them mad. Then I got indignant and threatened them with what I was going to do to them when I got loose. That didn't make them any friendlier. Then I just clammed up."

"Then what happened?"

Ron smiled again—grimly.

"Just what you'd expect, Doctor. They threw me in this damp drafty little cell in the basement and let me cool off for a couple of hours. Let's say I finally saw the logic of their arguments and applied for another interview. Everything went much better, and we finally straightened it all out. They were looking for *another* Ron who was also a professor and had a driver's license number one digit away from mine. We both looked a lot alike—beard and all. But it seems that my namesake was a little on the psychopathic side. He'd shot a narcotics agent a few months ago, and those cops were a little concerned that he might do some damage to them. Under the circumstances, I guess I made *all* the wrong moves!"

In Ron's case that was an understatement. Ron, impulsively, but understandably, violated every principle of conduct for dealing effectively with the police. What he did makes up an almost complete list of what you *shouldn't* do. Now let's see if we can make a list of what you *should* do.

1. *Be calm.* The fact that police officers come to visit you doesn't mean that they are going to arrest you. It may well be only an interview to obtain routine information about someone or something. Be polite, be casual, but be *alert*. There is no law that says you must give any information to a policeman that might possibly be against your own interest. *Listen* instead of talking until you find out exactly what is going on.

2. *Be firm.* Your rights are guaranteed under the Constitution. You cannot be forced to incriminate yourself; your property, home, and office are protected against illegal search and seizure; and the police are severely re-

stricted by Supreme Court decisions in what they can do to you.

3. *Be smart.* Politely and quietly ask the police officer if he is investigating you. If he says yes, *the interview should end right there!* The only further words you should say, from that point on, are these: *"I want an attorney."* Don't even comment on the weather. From that moment on anything you say can be hazardous to your health. The best strategy is to go into a kind of a trance. Do what the officers tell you, but don't say a word. If they allow you to call your lawyer from where you are, tell him or her only the following:

"There are some police officers here who want to question me. Will you please come over and be present, *immediately?"*

While you are waiting for your lawyer to arrive, do not engage in light conversation with the police. Remember, they are experts in dealing with people under pressure; don't give them a chance to work their tricks on you. It could come out all wrong. Just sit calmly and wait for your lawyer.

4. Be tough. If you insist on your constitutional rights, the police may well pressure you by threatening to arrest you. *That is all the more reason to keep absolutely silent.* If they're going to play hard ball, then you have to respond the same way. Remember what they read to you—and let's hope they *did* read it to you:

"THE LAW REQUIRES THAT YOU BE ADVISED THAT YOU HAVE THE RIGHT TO REMAIN SILENT, THAT ANYTHING YOU SAY CAN BE USED AGAINST YOU IN A COURT OF LAW, THAT YOU HAVE THE RIGHT TO THE PRESENCE OF AN ATTORNEY, AND THAT IF YOU CANNOT AFFORD AN ATTORNEY ONE WILL BE APPOINTED FOR YOU PRIOR TO ANY QUESTIONING IF YOU SO DESIRE."

That paragraph summarizes *some* but not *all* of your legal rights. Don't give them up! It's possible that if you don't answer the police officers' questions, they will in fact take you to the local jail. Don't let that intimidate you! Again, that's not exactly a fun trip, but you have to be tough and defend your rights to avoid worse trouble later on. If they are determined to take you in, like they say in the movies, ''go quietly.'' Refusing to answer questions is not a crime but resisting arrest *is*. Don't convert yourself into a criminal. The best attitude is the same trancelike state. Be cooperative but passive. If you haven't been allowed to call your lawyer, ask permission to do so again, but don't insist. Twice is enough. If they *don't* let you call your lawyer, *they* have committed a crime and probably nullified any legal process against you. So keep cool.

5. *Be brave.* Being arrested, being fingerprinted, being photographed, being locked in a cell are degrading and depressing. But you have to see them through. You should constantly keep in mind that being arrested is *not* being convicted and that there is a long legal process between you and any ultimate penalty. Once you have gotten in contact with your lawyer, your job is finished. The rest is up to him or her. That's why you should be careful to get the very best available lawyer under the circumstances. Criminal law is a highly specialized field, and the nice old attorney who wrote Uncle Joe's will last year is not the best choice. Get the best and sharpest criminal lawyer you can find; don't economize where your personal freedom is concerned. The Law is not sentimental; it doesn't care if you have five children and a big mortgage on your house and you have never even taken a cookie that didn't belong to you. Once you fall into the jaws of the massive law-enforcement meat grinder, you have to defend yourself as if your life depended on it—because it does!

6. *Be cheeful.* Being arrested is not the end of the world. You are not going to be forced to dress in black for the rest of your life nor are you going to have to live as an

outcast. As society expands and becomes more complicated, more and more honest citizens have unfortunate experiences with law-enforcement agencies. The important thing is to keep your head, make the right moves, and don't allow the circumstances to get you down. Questioning by the police doesn't mean arrest, arrest doesn't mean going to trial, and even trial doesn't mean conviction. So just take it step by step, and everything should come out all right.

Generally speaking, the same principles apply to most law-enforcement agencies although there are some exceptions. The Customs Service does have some special search privileges regarding your luggage and your person when you enter the United States. In spite of the usual prohibitions against search without a warrant or without reason to believe a crime has been committed, they can look through everything you have. They *cannot* trample any of your other constitutional guarantees in the process. The Immigration Service can ask you reasonable questions to determine your citizenship—but that's it. If you are entering the country and have trouble with an official of these agencies, simply ask to see the supervisor. A few words with him or her will usually set things straight. Remember, be polite, be relaxed, but be firm. Trouble comes from being too tough or being too weak.

The one law enforcement agency that you are most likely to have contact with is the traffic police. *Never argue with them!* Traffic officers are constantly exposed to danger, stress, and pressure. They can—and will—arrest you if you rub them the wrong way. The best strategy is simply to take the traffic ticket. If you are required to sign a statement saying that you will appear in court or that you have received the ticket, *sign it.* It isn't a confession of guilt. If you really aren't guilty, it is usually simple to defend yourself against traffic violations. Don't get locked up in jail over a minor traffic offense—it doesn't pay.

Next to a traffic policeman, as a law-abiding citizen you

are most likely to find yourself in contact with an agent of the Internal Revenue Service. Although you shouldn't panic, it's an event that you should take *very* seriously. There are complicated and very special laws and regulations that govern your relationship with the IRS—and most of them work against you. Furthermore, some of the things you may write on your tax return can be interpreted as federal criminal offenses. That isn't exactly chopped liver.

In addition to the regular IRS agent, there are also revenue agents whose job is to collect what the government says you owe them. You don't want to fool around with *them*. Even more menacing are the IRS employees known as "special agents." Their job is to investigate *criminal violations* of the tax laws. They are the elite of the IRS, and if they appear in your home or office, treat them as if they were electric eels. They are criminal police officers of the federal government, and you need to insist on each and every one of your constitutional safeguards. It is best *not* to answer their questions, not to show them any documents, and *not* to deal with them at all without the presence of your attorney.

In general, in tax matters you should have your attorney with you whenever you deal with an IRS inquiry. That applies to audits, interviews, and investigations. Don't try to economize under those circumstances. You will be playing a game in which you don't know the rules and in which your opponents are experts. You can only lose—unless you have a professional player on your team.

To summarize, these days anyone can get arrested, no matter how honest and law-abiding he or she is. The best way to turn a potential nightmare into a mere nuisance is to act with calmness, tact, and intelligence. Remember the rule "Be calm, be firm, be smart, be tough, be brave, and be cheerful." That's the way you'll always come out on top!

# 7
# Boredom

IN FRENCH, they spell it *ennui*. In Spanish, they spell it *aburrimiento*. In English, it's spelled "boredom." And in any language it spells *t-r-o-u-b-l-e*. Boredom is mental cancer—no more and no less. Probably more human disasters and tragedies spring from the bitterness of boredom than any other single condition. Henry's experience is typical.

Henry smiled. His smile was boyish and disarming—although Henry was more than a boy. He stood nearly six feet tall and wore the uniform of his trade. The shirt was brushed denim, the pants were soft pale suede, the sunglasses were mirrored aviator, and the butter-soft loafers were—what else?—Gucci. Around his neck there was a thin gleaming gold chain, and from the chain there dangled a tiny flat disk of gold.

"How's the record business, Henry?"

The smile flashed brighter.

"Nice to have a shrink who's with it, Doc."

"It's nice to have a patient who wears his profession around his neck, Henry. What seems to be the trouble?"

The smile slowly faded.

"Everything . . . and nothing."

53

Henry stood up and began to pace around the room. Suddenly he stopped in front of my desk and faced me.

"What do I do? What do I do? I've tried everything in the world to whip this boredom, and every day I get more and more bored. It's like I'm slowly drying up inside! Listen, Doc, I've got twenty-five best-selling record albums, ten gold records, and more money than I can ever spend, and it doesn't do a thing for me!"

Henry drew back the cuff of his shirt.

"See this watch? There are only two of them in the world. It's made from a platinum ruble coin from the court of the czars of Russia. It's all hollowed out inside and there's a complete digital movement with a solar activator. It cost me six thousand dollars and you know what—I can't even stand to look at it anymore!"

He pulled off the watch and threw it down on my desk—hard.

"You like cars, Doctor? Come over and see my collection. How about a 1938 Mercedes? Not those fiberglass cheapy imitations for twenty thousand or so. I've got the real thing —like it's fresh from the factory. Maybe you're a Rolls-Royce fan. Do you like the 1929 Silver Ghost? I've got two of those. Or maybe fire engines turn you on. I've got a 1923 Le France pumper, ready to go."

Henry turned and threw himself into a chair.

"I've tried everything, Doc. You name it, I've tried it!"

"Coke?"

Henry laughed.

"Cocaine? What kind do you mean? Bolivian? Peruvian? Colombian? Ecuadoran? I can tell 'em all by their taste. I don't think there's a drug I haven't tried. Listen, I've tripped on Angel Wings, CSD, TMT, Blue Fog, and Hong Kong Uppers."

"Hong Kong Uppers? What's that?"

Henry chuckled.

"You wouldn't be interested, Doc. It's not your bag. I've also done the two-legged drugs. You know, chicks.

There isn't a kind of girl that I haven't gone out with. I've been to the Forbidden Quarter of Tokyo. I had my houseboat in Kashmir. I even made it to the massage parlors of Bangkok. After a couple of days, I was bored stiff. Or more precisely, unstiff.

"You know what? I can't even stand to listen to records anymore, and that's my business. You like stereo? Come over and listen to mine sometime. I've got a twenty-four-track octaphonic unit with triple quartz turntables and a couple of stadium speakers—twenty-four-inch jobs with fourteen-pound magnets. I don't even turn it on anymore!"

"Where did you grow up, Henry?"

The smile came on again.

"Where everybody else in the record business grew up, Doc. In Brooklyn. My father had a candy store, and man, did I love to work there. I used to get there at seven in the morning on Saturdays to set the candy out. All those jaw breakers and sugar babies and those little wax teeth—you remember those? And those tiny ice cream cones and those long strips of paper with the candy dots glued on? And the paper always stuck to the candy?"

"Did you notice something, Henry?"

Henry's mouth fell open. He spoke slowly.

"Yeah, I sure did, Doc. You got me all enthusiastic. You know, maybe you're on to something. I never thought about it that way. After all, I wasn't *always* bored . . . ."

Obviously Henry's case is extreme—but only extreme in the depth of his boredom and his desperate and expensive attempts to entertain himself. But in every other way, his case is not much different from millions and millions of other apathetic and indifferent victims of boredom.

Boredom means a life that is drained of excitement and meaningful stimulation. It means a job that leads nowhere, that has no challenge and no real reward. Take Jeanie's job, for instance:

"I struggled four years to get where I am. I worked my

way up from secretary to copywriter in the hottest ad agency in New York and . . . and . . .''

"And what?"

Jeanie bit her lip.

"And . . . *I hate it!* I didn't put in four years of plotting and planning to write cute little ads for toilet bowl cleaners. I didn't spend four years studying creative writing in night school—sloshing through the rain and snow—to write copy for 'gentle laxatives.' Doctor, I'm so bored with my job *I could scream!*"

And well she could. And so could plenty of other Jeanies and Henrys around the country and around the world. As a matter of fact, boredom is so widespread that it has given birth to more than a dozen gigantic industries. What do you think television is all about? Commercial television is designed to give quick emotional "fixes" to millions of bored people. Situation comedies, police dramas, and other assorted offerings supply short twenty-two-minute doses (not including commercials) of intense plastic emotion, which acts as a cheap substitute for real experiences. The irony is that the great mass of bored people are even more bored by what they see on TV.

That's why television is electronic morphine. You have to keep increasing the concentration of the dose to maintain the effect. The comedy has to be more slapstick, the crime programs have to be more violent and sadistic, the sex has to be more explicit, or the bored viewers look elsewhere for relief. Sometimes they turn to the movies. The movies are bigger and brighter and louder than TV, and they can offer more emotional punch per presentation. The blood flows redder and faster, the sadomasochism is far more realistic, and movies get down to the real close-up pornography. But alas, even *that* becomes boring the second or third time around.

When the electronic drugs no longer hold boredom at bay, the temptation is to look to the chemical drugs. That's when the victims of boredom turn inward to what they call "the playground of my mind." It usually starts with mari-huana and/or uppers, downers, ludes, and booze and all the rest. Of course, that keeps boredom at bay only for a while, and then it's on to cocaine, heroin, hashish, and whatever other poison seems to be in fashion. That's usually the time when terminal boredom begins to set in since a mind that's clobbered by drugs develops an atten-tion span that can be measured in moments.

Of course, not everyone tries to flee boredom by zap-ping their minds. Some turn in desperation to material objects to keep them going. Those are the ones who have to have the latest digital watch or the latest stereo or the latest fashions, like Henry. If that doesn't work, they turn to old things like old cars or old furniture (antiques) or old paintings. But no matter whether their material objects are old or new, they run head on into the immutable Law of the Half-Life of Material Objects.

Think about it this way. You've always wanted a pool table. You've thought about it, planned for it, discussed it with your family. One day you finally decide to buy it. The first day it arrives you spend four hours—at least—playing pool. The next day you still love it, but it gets only about two hours of your time. The day after it's good for about an hour—and that's the way it is for the next week or so. Then your interest gradually wanes to half an hour a day, where it stays for a few months, later slowly decreasing. Finally, the pool table stands almost abandoned, and one fine day it finds its way into a dusty corner of the garage.

The same progression occurs with virtually almost any-thing you buy—computer games, videotape recorder, new watch, stereo, microwave oven. When you first think about buying it, it seems the ultimate answer to your boredom:

"We'll spend hours playing games on the computer!"

"That quadraphonic stereo is just what we need to fill our evenings!"

"A microwave oven will make cooking so much more exciting!"

That's what you think. It's fine in the beginning, but sooner or later the Law of the Half-Life of Material Objects takes over. What once fascinated you now bores you. What once you thought would fill your empty hours now fills your basement and your attic. All that wonderful and expensive hardware ends up hardly used and totally useless as a weapon against boredom.

It can even apply to human beings. Remember when you first meet someone new, how exciting and interesting they are? You think that they are finally going to make your life interesting and exciting. You can hardly wait for the first date. You look forward to the second date with *almost* the same anticipation—although not quite. The third, fourth, and fifth dates are okay. The sixth date is disappointing, and from then on it's downhill. That's when you make an amazing discovery. What you discover is this: In the case of those who suffer from boredom, the Law of the Half-Life of Material Objects applies equally well to human beings. You end up treating people just as if they were electronic toys destined to relieve your constant attacks of boredom.

Then the inevitable happens. In your new relationship, you coast for a while until one day the person that once excited you so much tells you: "You know, I hate to put it this way but *you bore me.*"

Of course, it may happen just the other way—when you reluctantly break the news to them that they bore *you.* But in any event, you're alone again—and bored again.

What's the solution? The solution is to analyze and understand what boredom is and what causes it. That's the only way you can finally overcome what amounts to a living death in which nothing entertains you and nothing satisfies you. Let's start right at the beginning.

1. *Boredom is a ravenous monster—don't feed him.* The big mistake that victims of boredom make is to try desperately to amuse themselves. That's where movies, TV,

video cassettes, detective novels, and all the rest find their market. But the more desperate you become to get "unbored," the more vulnerable you make yourself to that monster, *boredom*.

2. *Make your life interesting*. No matter where you are, no matter what you do, life is so full of opportunities for expansion and fulfillment that there should be no time to be bored. In the time of the czars, a Russian writer was exiled to Siberia. He lived alone in a miserable little hut in a frozen and desolate wasteland. He had no books, no letters, no diversions whatsoever. Night after frozen night he sat alone watching the stars. Finally he began charting their movements on scraps of paper. By the time his exile was lifted, half a dozen years later, he had made nearly a hundred important astronomical discoveries and begun a new career as a respected astronomer.

The most effective weapon against boredom is learning. Study anything but study something. Learn Spanish, learn French, learn Russian. Study welding, study music, study beekeeping. There is no knowledge that will not make you happier, more interested in life, and more interesting to other people. I have never found a person who regretted learning a new skill or a new language. Studying and sharing with other interesting and interested people is the way to banish boredom from your life forever.

3. *Don't take mental opium*. Starting right now, grit your teeth and swear off all the mental narcotics that so many people use to fight boredom. Stop watching television, don't waste those hours at trashy movies, forget about pulpy fiction. Filling your mind with that kind of pap only hastens softening of the brain. Those situation comedies, the awful soap operas, the sadism and violence that leap out at you from that little screen—they don't add anything to your life. And haven't you noticed something interesting? After four hours of watching television, you're more bored than ever before. Kick the mental opium habit and open your mind to a whole new world of possibilities.

4. *Give yourself something to look forward to*. That's the most powerful weapon in the war against boredom. Make sure that when you come home from work there's a project waiting for you. Make sure that when you wake up in the morning there's something to see or tend or study. Take the trouble to plan your weekends to make sure you don't end up in front of the idiot box—with idiots on both sides of the tube. Build something, plant something, learn something. But every day try to move ahead just a little bit intellectually, emotionally, creatively. The most exciting part of winning against boredom is that you only have to make a start. Once you launch yourself your momentum carries you on to accomplishments you never even dreamed possible.

5. *You weren't always bored*. Remember the case of Henry. When his life was simpler, when he worked in his father's little candy store in Brooklyn, there were plenty of things that excited and interested him. You *make* yourself bored, and in the same way you can un-bore yourself. But you have to take positive, and sometimes drastic, action. If your job bores you to death, change it. If your friends bore *you*, maybe it's your problem. But if they are all bored themselves, run away from them because *boredom is a contagious disease and you can catch it!* Do whatever you have to do to ignite that lost spark of interest in yourself and in life itself. Unless you do you are as good as dead.

Start to work right now, today. Stop trying to kill time to get away from boredom. Look at it this way: You can never really kill time because while you're trying to do it, time is killing *you*. Think about it.

# 8
# Burnout

BURNOUT. Nowadays, everyone knows what that means. It's the all-too-familiar case of bright young men or women who start from the bottom, work terribly hard, make tremendous sacrifices, and finally one day zoom upward like a rocket. They soar to the top of their career or profession in a dazzling blaze of glory and then, just like a rocket, they burn out and come crashing down to earth! Tom is a good example.

Tom tipped back in his chair and slipped his thumbs into the waistband of his faded blue jeans—the *unfashionable* brand. He wore a nondescript blue gray sweater and nondescript tennis shoes. In fact, everything about Tom was nondescript except for his penetrating brown eyes and his obvious intelligence.

"I know what you're thinking, Doctor. You're wondering how this weird character is going to come up with the money to pay your bill."

"That's not exactly what was on my mind, Tom. I was actually wondering what kind of uniform you used to wear."

"What do you mean?"

"Well, Tom, the only educated people who dress like

61

you do are the ones who hate the uniform they used to wear.''

Tom smiled and the lines around his eyes crinkled. He wasn't quite so young as his outfit implied, more forty-five than thirty-five. He pulled a wrinkled color snapshot out of his back pocket and tossed it on my desk.

''I guess I came to the right place, Doctor. It's a shot of me in my full dress uniform as a Corporate Carpet Colonel, New Products Battalion, Detergent and Wax Regiment. At that moment I was living '*Operation Glitter-Wax*' twenty-four hours a day. We'd already test-marketed our new secret weapon—a floor wax that was cheaper and not much worse than all the rest. Look at the expression on my face; see how happy I am?''

The picture showed a man dressed in a blue suit, a striped tie, and a pastel shirt. His hair was cropped short. He was sitting behind a gigantic desk in a luxurious office talking on the telephone and glaring into the camera. He looked tense and grim—not to mention angry.

''Doc, that was taken about six months ago; the very next day I went upstairs to the Corporate Commanding General, the Chairman of the Board, and turned in my sword. I was earning—no, that's wrong. They were *paying* me, including bonuses and stock plans and all that, just under two hundred thousand dollars a year.''

''Why did you quit?''

Tom smiled again.

''You know the answer to that, don't you Doctor? One morning I woke up and discovered that I was just about to be turned into another *new product*. I was on the verge of becoming '*Mr. Glitter-Wax*'—Executive-of-the-Year— slaving sixty-five hours a week to make gooey wax to gum up the nation's floors.''

Tom raised his hand.

''No, that's not all of it. I suddenly realized that there was more to life than promoting cheap wax and thinking I was really doing something worthwhile. And I don't necessarily mean worthwhile for the world—I mean worthwhile for *me*. After all, that's what life is all about, isn't it?''

''Yes, that's what life is all about.''

Tom's problem isn't unique. More and more people every day are burning out. Maybe you're one of them—or maybe you're married to one of them. If so, you know the symptoms:

1. *The wake-up experience*. Burnouts describe it like this: ''One morning I woke up and decided I just couldn't make it to that office ever again.'' Or they say, ''I was talking to a client on the telephone, and I suddenly woke up and realized that wasn't what I wanted to do all my life.''

2. *The success syndrome*. Burnouts are almost always successful in their field of endeavor—that's what burns them out. They have everything—financial success, recognition, fancy cars, expensive houses. Let Glenn tell it.

Glenn is tall, tanned, and tailored. His pale beige safari suit fits as if it were glued directly onto his muscular body. As he talks, he ticks off the words on his fingers, almost as if he were saying a nursery rhyme: ''Lamborghini, Gucci, Dunhill? Beverly Hills, Dior, Aquascutum? Palm Beach, Cartier, Rosenthal! Rolex, Wedgwood, Tiffany! Monte Cristo, Bally, Lalique? You know what those words mean, Doctor?''

He answered his own question, again counting on his fingers: ''Nothing—nothing—and—*nothing*. It's the bait on the fishhook to catch suckers like me. I traded twenty years of my life for the 'right' brands and the 'right' addresses. I had to burn out to wake up.''

3. *Burnouts are smart*. If they weren't, they wouldn't zoom high enough and fast enough to burn out. Of course, their intelligence is their saving grace; we'll see about that in a minute or two.

Okay, the question is, Are *you* a burnout? Let's find out, and if you are, let's see what we can do about it.

One of the real problems about choosing a career is that you usually have to make the choice long before you have any idea what it's all about. If you're going to be a doctor, you have to decide at about the age of eighteen. Then you have to resign yourself to all those long years of pre-med, medical school, internship, specialty training, and all the rest. By the time you find out what it's *really* like to be a doctor, it's too late to turn back. (If you don't believe me, ask *any* doctor.) The same holds true for law, accounting, dentistry, and most other careers. One of the biggest surprises comes in the area of business. Let's listen again to Glenn.

"When I was growing up, you know what I wanted to be most of all, Doctor? I wanted to be an *executive!* That was a magic word for me: 'executive.' Wow! I had visions of board meetings, tense decisions, executive suites, midnight flights to exotic places. Well, I got my MBA from Harvard, I worked my tail off for ten years, and I finally got to be a *senior* executive! You can't get any higher than that!"

Glenn smiled ironically.

"And you know what? I made a tremendous discovery— actually the most important discovery of my life. I discovered that 'executive' is just a fancy name for a manager, an administrator, a very, very smart clerk. An executive is someone who takes care of somebody else's business for them. The president of the company—or as they like to call it these days, the CEO, the chief executive officer—is just another employee."

"When did you discover that, Glenn?"

Glenn chuckled.

"Nine years, eleven months, and twenty-one days too late. It hit me like a ton of bricks the day I celebrated ten years with the Atlantic-Freestone International Corporation. By coincidence that was the day they made me president of the company. A month later I burned out and here I am."

When you realize that your job isn't really what you expected it to be, you're already halfway down the road to burning out. The other half is a matter of rewards. Juanita is an expert on that subject.

She is tall, olive-skinned, with dark eyes and an exotic beauty that is barely muted by her executive uniform. She wears a beige pleated skirt, an off-white silk blouse with a blue and gold patterned silk scraf, and a navy blue blazer. Her voice is low and sexy:

"Of course, you know it's much harder for a woman. I gave up a lot to go into business for myself. And I suppose you know how terribly competitive the cosmetics business is, Doctor. But it was very important to me, and you'll never believe how much I sacrificed. And now I have everything—a Rolls-Royce, a company plane, apartments in London and Paris, anything I want. Sometimes I can't believe it. I can go into any shop anywhere in the world and buy any dress I want! I don't even have to ask the price in advance! And when I was a little girl working in my father's luncheonette, this was all beyond my fondest dreams. And . . . and now. Do you know what, Doctor?"

Juanita looked at me plaintively.

"What, Juanita?"

The tears welled up in her big beautiful eyes.

"For the past six months, the same five letters have been going around in my head, over and over again. *I-T-A-T-I. I-T-A-T-I. I-T-A-T-I.* It's like a tattoo. I can't get it out of my mind. Do you know what those letters stand for, Doctor? *Do you know what they stand for?*"

The tears were rolling down Juanita's cheeks now.

"They stand for *Is that all there is?* That's what they stand for! I invested the best eleven years of my life in my business, Doctor. I'm thirty-seven years old now. I have *everything* that comes with what they call "success" and all I can think of is, *is that all there is?* Is that all there is?"

When the *is that all there is?* tattoo gets into your head, you're close to the end of the line. Now what do you do? You burn out, of course. But you burn out constructively. Just as you went up the ladder by being smart and creative, you go not down, but horizontally, in a smart and creative way. When the moment arrives that you hate your job, your surroundings, your co-workers, everything about the career that was once so important to you, what's the first thing you do? The first thing you do is:

1. *Nothing*. You take plenty of time to think and analyze and make sure that you *really* hate your present way of life. You make sure that it's not something else that's upsetting you. After all, you don't want to turn everything upside down just because you had a bad day with your boss. On the other hand, if you don't want to have a boss—ever again—then it's time to move on to step number two.

2. *Leave—and then do nothing*. Life is too short to waste doing something you hate. The truth is that you don't *really* burn out, you burn yourself free! There are tens of thousands of cases of men and women who leave the competitive corporate rat races to do their own thing. On the other hand, how many people do you know who gave up independent individualistic lives to become corporate executives? Once you burn yourself free, your next challenge is to find the right place in the scheme of things for you and your talents.

3. *Make peace with your family first*. They were part of your decision to follow the course that burned you out. Now they should be part of your new life too. You can benefit from their enthusiasm and insights, and you'll find that you will develop a whole new relationship with them in the process. You may be amazed and delighted when you get to know what your wife and children are really like.

4. *Make sure that you do what you really like*. Don't exchange one bad deal for another. If you have to lower

your standard of living to start enjoying your life, so what? All those great brand names didn't do anything for Glenn and they didn't do anything for you.

Sometimes it pays to get away to another world for a while to clear all that "success" trash out of your head. Maybe buy a sailboat and sail around the world or move to another country for a year or so. If you live in the city, don't be afraid to move to a ranch or farm. That's where *all* of us came from in the beginning anyway. Cities are a relatively new development for the human race. Changing your surroundings will expand your mind, open new horizons, and confirm what you always suspected. The middle-class American road to happiness may not be *your* road to happiness. There are over four billion people on this planet, and most of them get more out of life than the folks in Middle America. You don't believe me? Okay, check it out for yourself. That's the whole idea.

5. *Burning out is not the end, it's the beginning.* Actually it's the greatest opportunity of your lifetime. It's the moment when you have the best of both worlds. You have the accumulated experience of all the past years plus the incentive to put that experience to work in your new way of life. When you look at it that way, burning out is the best thing that ever happened to you! Enjoy it!

# 9
# Children

CHILDREN, CHILDREN, CHILDERN! They're always a problem. First you have to go through the nuisance of being a child yourself, then you have to have your own children, then you have to bring them up—then they grow up and move away and you have to worry about them. One of the greatest sources of anxiety in dealing with children is the anxiety that comes from having to make the hundreds of decisions in relation to them. And the first decision about children is probably the most difficult one: should you have any?

I think the answer is yes more often than it is no. I'm aware of all the antichildren propaganda that's been going around lately—about how children interfere with careers and fulfillment and all that sort of thing. To tell you the truth, I'm not impressed with any of it. I think most of it comes from people who are *afraid* to have children themselves. Why should they be afraid? Because having a child is the true test of your success in the role of an adult. It works like this:

Up until the moment that you have your own child, you can function like a child yourself. All of your attention is focused on *you*—*your* needs, *your* feelings, *your* clothes, *your* friends, *your* career, *your* whims, and *your* impulses. Until the moment that you have your own children, you can be a lifelong child—playing games, collecting toys, acting out childish fantasies. Of course, if you're an adult child, we call the games "sports," the toys "accessories," and the childish fantasies are known as "life-style." When you have a child you have to give all that up—and sometimes it hurts. But you get a lot in return.

What you get is the opportunity for two of the greatest satisfactions that a human being can experience. You are allowed unlimited *projection* and unlimited *undoing*. These are privileges that are not available in any other area of your life. If you have a child—and you love your child— you are allowed to *project* your own image onto that child. That is to say, you transfer your own feelings and wishes and hopes onto a little person who is the extension and duplication of you yourself. You can give to that child everything that *you* wanted and were denied when you were a child. You can make that little life better in every way than the life that you had when you were little. Of course, there are hazards involved.

Some parents try to project their unfulfilled desires too directly and too obviously onto their children. Those are the kids who get ten-speed bicycles and electric trains at the age of two, who have baby wardrobes that cost a fortune, who are overwhelmed with material possessions. That's not the best expression of *projection*. The most rewarding opportunity is the chance to give your child the warmth and love and fulfillment that you yourself were denied as a little one. The greatest opportunity that all parents have is *to make a better life for their child than they had when they were small*. And that doesn't mean fancy plastic tea sets and supersized teddy bears and French provincial baby furniture. It means love and affection and understanding without limit—like you probably never had when you were growing up. And that brings us to the next opportunity: *undoing*.

Life is not always easy, especially when you're a child. (I'm sure you've noticed.) We've all had experiences when we were growing up that we would prefer had never happened. Yet there's no way to erase those unpleasant moments—or years, in some cases. Once they make their impression on us, that impression is there forever. Or is it? Well, there's a way to dissolve the most unpleasant times of our childhood once and for all. There's a way to expunge them almost magically from our unconscious— and conscious—minds. That magic is called *undoing*.

Here's how it works. Say your mother—or father—was always too busy to pay attention to you. It was always the housework or your brothers or sisters or the demands of the job or something. You grew up isolated and at a distance from your parents. You didn't like it. It left its indelible mark upon you. Well, that mark doesn't have to be so indelible. You can turn back the clock and *undo* those years of rejection and indifference. How? Well, with your own children. By providing them with warmth and love, by never being too busy to spend a spare moment with them, by sharing your life with them as your parents never shared their lives with you, you can replace that empty space in your own life with love and satisfaction. And the only way you can ever accomplish that magic is with your own children. Helping out with other people's kids, pampering a pet poodle, doing volunteer work at the local orphanage just won't do the trick.

So, in addition to any other considerations, the satisfactions that come from projection and undoing are very important reasons to have your own children. I think they are more important than so-called freedom, more important than a career, more important than having money to spend on the latest material trinket. Make your own decision, as always, but be sure to take *all* the facts into consideration.

Once you have your own child—or children—things are not going to be perfect. There will be—or there already are —moments when you will literally and actively *hate* your kids. You will hate them because they have deprived you of something you are convinced you should have. If you are a woman, they will perhaps deprive you of your flat little tummy that you were always so proud of. At the same time, having a baby etches little stretch lines across your girlish abdomen. And being a mother means a lot of extra work. It means midnight feedings, it means diapers everywhere, it means staying up night after night with a sick baby.

Being a father means losing out on a lot of sexual satisfaction with your wife. Be honest. During the last few months of pregnancy, during the first few months after delivery when the baby is crying all night, there is little if any sex. It also means extra worry, extra expense, and extra responsibility.

For both husband and wife, having a child means a lot of sacrifices. You can't buy all the things you want, you can't always travel the way you would like to travel, you can't always dress and entertain the way you would like to. The money and time and energy that you could once dedicate to yourself, you now have to devote to your children. Wait, there's more. Children also have a habit of being naughty. "Naughty" is a nice word we use instead of the word we really mean. The word we really mean is "*bad*." We could also use words like "hateful," "rotten," "destructive," "mean," "vicious," and just plain "awful." Because that's really how it is. When your two year old takes his drinking glass and throws it on the floor, that's not naughty. That's *bad*. When your teen-ager wipes out your new car, that's not naughty, that's *destructive*. When your five year old carves up your butcher-block dining room table with a screwdriver, that's not naughty, that's *mean*. We use the word "naughty" to help us pretend that children are not capable of badness and to help us control—or pretend to control—our hatred and resentment toward our children when they are *bad*. But the truth is that just like adults, sometimes kids are just plain old *b-a-d*.

It's the accumulation of thousands of those experiences over a period of twenty years or so that makes parents so bitter, that alienates them from their children, and that takes so much of the pleasure out of being a parent. What to do about it? Well, there's another magic word. It's called *identification*.

Identification is the ability—or perhaps a better word is the "talent"—to transplant yourself symbolically into the mind and body of your child. For a few moments you see things exactly the way he sees them. You react exactly the way he reacts. You feel exactly the way he feels. When your two year old throws his drinking glass on the floor, instead of seeing it as an act of aggression directed at you, you develop the abiliy to understand—at least in part— how he felt and what impelled him to do it. Was it because an indifferent mother (you!) served him the same awful baby food three days in a row? Was it because he has to eat lunch alone every day? Was it because he's jealous of the attention heaped on his new baby sister?

Whatever the cause, the important thing for you to realize is *there was a cause!* No behavior—including the behavior of children—occurs at random. There is a reason— however deeply buried—for every human act. In the case of children you usually don't have to look very deep to see what's behind it.

If your teen-ager wrecks your new car, ask yourself what he's trying to tell you. Put yourself in his place and try to *feel* what's going on in his life. Ask what made him so desperate that he risked his life to send you a message. You may be amazed at the kinds of answers you find. When your five year old slashes your expensive dining room table with that big screwdriver, instead of lunging at him with a sledgehammer, try to climb inside his skin and feel what impelled him to such a drastic deed.

There's another advantage to *identification* with your

children. If you identify with them, you will always make the right decisions, since you will have access to their thoughts and feelings and your own as well. Let's take some examples to see how it can work:

I. *Should your seventeen-year-old daughter go two thousand miles away to a big city college?* Here are the facts: The girl is an only child, very bright, and attached to her parents. She has a scholarship to a prestigious university to study anthropology. She's eager to start her career, but as the time to leave home approaches she becomes more and more depressed. What should you do?

1. Depression is just part of cutting the umbilical cord. Treat the situation as matter-of-factly as you can and bundle her off to school.

2. Send her to a psychiatrist to get her emotional problems under control before she starts college life.

3. Explain to her that you just can't afford to send her to college unless she accepts the scholarship and goes far away.

4. Confront her with all the sacrifices you have made for her and let her know she's letting you down.

II. *What should you do about your six-year-old boy who still wets the bed?* No matter how many times you wake him during the night, the bed is still wet in the morning. This has been going on for the past six months. What should you do?

1. Get one of those new electronic machines that gives him an electric shock every time he wets the bed.

2. Don't give him any liquid to drink after 3:00 P.M. no matter how much he cries.

3. Take him to a psychiatrist to find out what his mental problem is.

4. Just pretend it isn't happening.

\*   \*   \*

III. *What should you do about your three-year-old boy who just doesn't want to eat?* Almost everything you offer him gets thrown on the floor; he cries when you try to force him to eat, and yet he seems healthy and maintains his weight. What should you do?

1. Take him to the pediatrician for a complete physical exam and extensive laboratory tests to see if he has a physical disease.

2. Don't let him get up from the table until he eats what you think he should.

3. Make him take plenty of vitamins and minerals and protein supplements to make sure he's getting enough nutrition.

4. Spank him if he won't eat what you give him.

If you've read this far, it shouldn't be hard to guess the correct answers to these three questions. Here they are:

I. *1. wrong 2. wrong 3. wrong 4. wrong*

II. *1. wrong 2. wrong 3. wrong 4. wrong*

III. *1. wrong 2. wrong 3. wrong 4. wrong*

The one *right* answer to each of these questions is simple: To decide what to do to solve each of these problems, *identify* with your children. Ask yourself how they feel, what impels them to do the strange things that they are doing, and, the most important question of all, *what urgent message are they sending you with their behavior?*

Once you get the answer to those questions, you'll find it's actually easy to do what's best for your children and for your family. As your mastery of the art of identification improves, you'll be amazed that your relationship with your children will become a source of constant pleasure and gratification and satisfaction—to you and to them. And after all, that's what you want, isn't it?

# 10
# Depression

SO YOU'RE FEELING DEPRESSED? Congratulations, that's exactly what you wanted. Hey, hang on a minute! What's that all about? How can anyone *want* to be depressed? Depression is terrible! Depression is torture! Who wants *that?*

Everyone who is depressed wants *that*. Where do you think depression comes from, Outer Space? Every depression every human being has ever had comes from exactly the same place—the Inner Space that sits on the end of his or her neck. Depression begins and *ends* in the human brain. *And that's the good news!* Because if that's so, then we can figure out how to stop it and maybe even how to prevent it. As far as stopping it is concerned, *before you finish reading this chapter your depression will subside*. Notice I said "subside"—not disappear by magic once and for all. Why? Because *you* produced that depression, and it's going to take time before you're really willing to give it up. But let's not get ahead of ourselves.

Most depressions have several characteristics in common. Perhaps most important is the *pain*. Depression *hurts*. It feels like someone is twisting both your arms and both your legs—mentally. You have an unbearably heavy weight pressing down on your entire being. Everything is blotted out except feelings of doom and destruction. Your consciousness is flooded with images of all the bad things that are going to happen to you. Sound familiar? Okay. But hang on.

Depressions all have an element of *fantasy*. *Most of the time*—not always—the things you are so depressed and fearful about never occur! That's true. Think back, if you can, to the reasons for the last three episodes of depression you had. What's that? You can't remember? Huh? Just a minute. Isn't that a little suspicious? The imminent disasters that you feared so desperately—the ones that plunged you into the pits of depression—you can't even remember what they were? Of course you can't because the whole experience was *phoney*. That's what I said: *p-h-o-n-e-y*. A depression is a little soap opera written, produced, directed by—and starring—*you*. Like most soap operas it has almost nothing to do with reality. Its primary purpose is to take your mind off the real problems that threaten you. Is there a little light at the end of the tunnel? I thought so. Let's push on.

Another universal characteristic of depression is the flood of accusations that it brings. Most—but not all—depressions are triggered by a chance event in reality. You had a fight with your best friend. The shares of stock you bought just went down. You got fired from your job. You husband told you that you're getting too fat. The first thing that happens is *nothing*. There is a period of from one hour to one day in which you don't really feel bad. You deny the importance of the problem, you deny any responsibility for it, and you deny any future repercussions. Then when the period of grace is over, the floodgates of depression open wide and engulf you! The first—and worst—event is *accusations*. A torrent of hateful accusations comes pouring down on your head. You got fired from your job? Okay, now hear this:

1. "You're a stupid incompetent!" That accusation is

followed by a list of jobs you have been fired from—
beginning back in high school if not earlier.

2. "You fooled them for a while but they finally caught
on to you!" Then comes a list of more of the things in life
you *thought* you got away with but actually didn't.

3. "You'll never get another job!" This tirade is full of
fantasies about how your past employer will blackball you
with any possible future employer and make all your desperate job seeking fruitless. Sometimes, if you're lucky
(?), the flood of accusations admits that you might possibly find future employment but only under certain conditions.
If you were vice-president of a manufacturing company,
the forces of depression might generously concede that
someone could take pity on you and put you in charge of
the men's washroom.

Did you notice something interesting? I said "the forces
of depression." What's that all about? It's about this:
Inside every human being is a terrible destructive force
lurking just under the surface with one goal and one goal
only—to cause the maximum amount of suffering in the
minimum amount of time. As soon as this destructive
force—let's call it D.F. for short—finds the tiniest chink
in your armor, the smallest breakdown of your defenses, it
goes to work on you—with no mercy whatsoever! It pulls
the roof down on your head. It throws every dish in the
kitchen straight at you. It kicks and spits and gouges like
fifty wildcats *to make you suffer*. Worst of all, it has every
one of your innermost secrets at its disposal. It knows all
of your little (and not so little) sins. It knows all those
naughty little things you've done—*and with whom*. Most
important of all, it knows all the forbidden things you'd
like to do. And it punishes you for each and every one of
them. It knows every bad grade you ever got in school. It
knows every time you've been rejected by a girl friend or a
boyfriend. It knows every mistake you've ever made. It
knows about every experience—however insignificant—
you've ever had with drugs, abortion, homosexuality,

stealing, sex, drinking, and every other little human pecca-
dillo that ever existed. It uses your own life experiences,
your own mind, and your own energy against you. That's
what depression is—no more and no less. *It's you against
you.* Knowing that, you can stop it. And you will.

One of the simplest, most effective, and most neglected
weapons against depression is the "hat trick." All you
have to do is think of your depression as if it were a hat,
sitting on your head. If you consider it for a moment, that
isn't far from the truth. Depression *is not a part of your
life.* It's merely something that sits on top of your mind—
very much like a big, ugly, and unwanted hat. The solution?
Grab that hat, pull it off, and throw it as far as you can!
Take that awful, oppressive, unbearable feeling of depression and throw it as far away as you can! Try it—it works.
Why? Because it seizes upon the undeniable fact of reality
that *your fate and your future life are not determined by
your temporary feelings of desperation.* Take off your
ugly, awful depression hat and throw it away, and you will
suddenly be amazed at how well you feel, how well you
function, and how well you are able to deal with the very
problems that produced the depression in the first place!

Another superb and effective antidote to depression is
hard work. The destructive force within you really needs
to have you cornered to give you the works. If you're
slumped in a chair in a dark corner wallowing in self-pity,
it has you right where it wants you. But if you are doing
something constructive, something active, it has to back
off. The proof? Well, just reading this chapter makes you
feel better because *you are doing something about your
problem.* Your D.F. hates a moving target! So, do the
wash, chop wood, wax the car, paint your house, clean out
the garage—but *do something!* The harder you work, the
more physical energy you will expend, and the less depressed you will feel. I know you may not feel like
working, but force yourself to do something—the more
strenuous the better. Once you get started you will be

amazed! Hard physical work actually deprives your D.F. of the energy it needs to work *against* you. Try it—you'll be amazed!

These two techniques—the "hat trick" and "stealing" the energy from your D.F. so it can't use your energy against you—are superb techniques for stopping an acute episode of depression. The next question—and I can hear you asking it—is how to prevent depression in the first place.

To be honest, the answer to that question is beyond the scope of my *Mental First-Aid Manual!* Depression is a complex emotional problem that has to be dealt with in a comprehensive way. *But* there are certain things that everyone can do to help prevent depressions from beginning in the first place. Here are some things that are sure to help.

1. *Remember that depression has nothing to do with what's really going on.* As we have seen, in depression the tremendous flood of threats and accusations is all out of proportion to what is really happening. To put it another way, a minor disappointment in one's daily routine is the *excuse* for your inner destructive force to hit you with every defect you've had in your entire life.

2. *Don't try to cut corners.* Honesty is not the *best* policy—it's the *only* policy. You give your inner destructive force a golden opportunity to attack you when you try to cut financial, sexual, emotional, or moral corners. There is no such thing as a free lunch. You can't cheat your customers, lie to your wife or husband, or take a few drugs from time to time and expect to escape the inevitable retribution of that vicious enemy that lives inside your head. I'm sorry that's the way it is, but I didn't make the rules—I can only tell you what they are.

3. *Try not to preside at your own funeral.* That means, don't *help* your inner destructive force to *hurt* you. When it starts to launch a depressive attack against you, don't just stand there and take it. Don't believe its threats of destruc-

tion as if they were the gospel truth. Don't wallow in those wonderful images of defeat that it inflicts on you. Don't believe its horrible predictions of the future. You can stand up on your hind legs and fight back! You can answer it back like this: "How come you're so sure that everything is going to turn out so badly?" Or "Why are you telling me all these exciting things?" Or "Just go to hell!"

Sometimes it even helps to say these things out loud so your D.F. can hear them loud and clear. And here's one final point that's very important to keep in mind. *You don't have to be depressed if you don't want to be depressed. You have the power to say, "I simply refuse to be depressed!"* It works. Try it and you'll see. Good luck.

# 11
# Divorce

OFFHAND, I can think of only two positive aspects to getting a divorce:

1. In many marriages, getting divorced may be the first thing that husband and wife have *ever* agreed on.

2. It's very difficult to have a really good marriage, but it's easy to have a good divorce.

And that's what this chapter is about: how to have a decent, humane, nontraumatic divorce. When you really come down to' it, if a marriage has been nothing but unhappiness for a man and a woman and the solution they both agree on is divorce, that's the moment the suffering should *stop*. The terrible boxing match between Siamese twins that makes up so many disastrous marriages is over. It's time to separate once and for all—physically, mentally, emotionally and spiritually. The emotional volcano has erupted, and now is the moment for the two survivors to pick up the pieces of their lives and start over.

That's not what everybody does. All too many people use divorce as an opportuniy for a long-playing emotional orgy. They simply move the private disaster of their marriage to the public arena—the courts, the newspapers, and the laps of their unfortunate friends. How do you spell *divorce?* Easy. You spell it *e-n-d*. That's all she wrote. It's all over. *F-i-n-i-s-h-e-d.*

If you want to have a successful divorce constantly keep that word in mind: *e-n-d.* Repeat it to yourself every time you have to deal with any of the million details of disentangling yourself and your life from another human being with whom you have tried to fuse over the course of many years. *E-n-d. F-i-n-i-t-o. F-i-n-i-s-h-e-d. O-v-e-r.* Let every encounter with your ex-spouse (or soon-to-be ex-spouse) be a period instead of a comma. Let it be the chance to cut one more tie, to wrap up one more loose end, to put more distance between you.

Once you have decided to get a divorce—and be *sure* that's what you want—do everything you can to make it swift and painless. My own personal feeling is that a big leap forward is to stay away from lawyers. I don't have anything against lawyers. But lawyers—by definition—are hired guns, mercenaries. They are paid to go to war for their clients. And the last thing that a man and a woman who have suffered through years of a rotten marriage need is more *war!* They've had enough. The truth is that a spouse who hires a tough lawyer to contest a bitter divorce *doesn't want a divorce.* He or she wants to maintain at least some kind of emotional contact with his or her now-estranged mate. There is actually a greater chance for reconciliation among couples who want to fight like tigers over the divorce. Sound strange? It shouldn't. It's only undeniable evidence that there is still a powerful emotional bond between them. Amazing as it may sound, that bond can sometimes be restructured to provide a basis for a happy and lasting marriage!

But let's assume that you're really through as husband and wife—once and for all. Then what you're involved in is a simple salvage operation. The great ocean liner of your marriage has sunk, and you want to save as many items of value as possible to enable the two of you to start new lives. That's really what it's all about. Don't be tempted to try to steal some of the salvage that really should go to your ex-spouse. You'll only motivate him or her to do the same thing to you—and that's the war we're trying to avoid.

The first order of business is *money*. In some places it's relatively easy. If community-property laws apply, half of everything the marriage has acquired goes to each spouse. Just sit down and divide it right down the middle as if you were splitting up somebody else's property. And while you're doing it, remember you have a tremendously powerful incentive to work it out between you. That incentive is simply this: If you can't agree, you'll have to go to the lawyers. That means one law firm for the wife and one for the husband. You can assume that each law firm will take at least 10 percent of the property in fees—if things go very smoothly. If the battle drags out, as much as 20 percent or more can go to each firm. A couple who has accumulated $100,000 in wealth over the years ends up with only $60,000 to split between them. So by being reasonable and not too greedy, each spouse stands to gain, tax-free, as much as $20,000 cold cash. Keep that in mind when you're arguing over who gets the sofa.

If you don't happen to live in community-property territory, you have ten times the incentive to make a fast, fair, and private settlement between the two of you. You see, without the community-property rules to go by, the lawyers have no guidelines and it's every man's lawyer for himself. Those are the divorce cases that eat up every last cent in legal fees and court costs. In a sense they solve the problem once and for all. After a few years of haggling you don't have to worry about a settlement—there's nothing left! So dividing everything right down the middle quickly and privately makes the best sense overall in virtually every case.

Child support shouldn't be a problem either. After all, the children are *your* children. And *they* didn't mess up the marriage—you did. With their mother and father divorced, they're going to have enough problems without you adding a few more. It goes without saying that mother shouldn't try to inflate child support payments to give her a little extra spending money. Why not? Simple. If the payments are too high, the husband just won't come up with the money. The old days of locking up men for nonpayment are fading fast. The idea of equality between the sexes and new social philosophies make it less and less likely for judges to squeeze the last drop out of ex-husbands. And the man who wants to disappear can do it more easily now than ever.

The question of alimony falls into the same category. A smart woman really doesn't want alimony because it acts as an emotional crutch that prevents her from launching herself into her new life. Alimony is the undeniable evidence that she still needs the husband that she thought she could do without. If it's at all possible to get along without alimony, it's better for everyone concerned. However, in some cases alimony can be a real help for a year or so to make the transition from one way of living to another less painful. But the days of getting paid for investing the "best years of my life" with a man are nearly over. Most likely the best years are going to come *after* you set yourself free from him.

When it comes to visiting rights and privileges, don't try to get even that way either because you'll only be getting even with yourself. If a mother gets custody of a child fifty weeks out of the year and the father gets to see his offspring only 14 days out of 365, the mother might feel some grim satisfaction. That satisfaction will quickly fade when her child takes revenge on her for making him or her grow up without a father. You may hate your ex-spouse, but you don't hate your kids, do you?

Okay, then don't take it out on them. In exactly the same way, the temptation for a man to try to prove that his ex-wife is what lawyers call ''an unfit mother'' may seem appealing. But please resist that temptation. In this crazy world children need everything a father can give them *and* everything a mother can give them—and then some. Even if the father isn't perfect and even if the mother has her problems, it's better for children to have as much time as possible with each parent than to struggle through the problems of growing up with half their team missing.

Another source of damage in the salvage operation known as divorce comes from the barracudas that swim around the wreckage. Those are the friends and relatives who tell you what to do and how to do it. Here are the ways they'll sink you every time:

1. *"You mean you're going to let him get away with that!"* That's designed to whip you into a frenzy and make you tear your ex-mate to pieces. Think of it this way—what you want to do is get away from an awful marriage with your brain and body intact, and the faster and easier you can do it the better.

2. *"But you have a right to the children!"* We already went over that. And the children have a right to both their parents. And you have a right to tell people like that to mind their own business.

3. *"But after all you did for him (or her)!"* Yes, and after all you did *to* him (or her). Look, a ruined marriage is a combination of good times and bad times and it just so happens that you feel the bad times won out. You don't have to justify what you're doing to anyone. The biggest job at hand is simply to get yourself untangled.

Let's be honest. At best, getting a divorce is mind-bruising, harrowing, traumatic, expensive, and terribly destructive for everyone involved—husband, wife, and children. By using superhuman exertion and following all of the suggestions in this chapter, you can minimize the agony. On the other hand, if you're going to go to all that trouble, maybe it's easier to devote all that energy to putting your marriage back together again! Think about it.

# 12
## Envy

ENVY is the most corrosive of all human emotions and at the same time the most exquisitely painful of all self-tortures. In a real sense it's like observing everyone else through an immense magnifying glass and looking at yourself through the wrong end of a telescope. What other people have, what they do, what they accomplish, all looks bigger than life. To say the least, your own accomplishments seem miniature by comparison. Peter is a typical case:

"I wonder if I'm getting anywhere, Doctor. I seem to have spent the last twenty years on a treadmill."

Peter brushed some imaginary lint off the lapel of his well-cut suit, then went on.

Look, this is the problem. I have a good business. I import electronics parts, and every year for the past ten years we've done better than the year before. I have a nice house on two acres with a couple of horses. I have two kids—age eight and ten—and a great wife. We belong to a fairly good country club, and we go to Europe every year. We have three cars and some pretty good investments."

Peter paused.

"That's fine, Peter. But what's the problem?"

Peter lunged forward in his chair.

*"The problem? The problem? Don't you see? That is the problem! I'm not getting anywhere!"*

"Take it easy, Peter. Can you be more precise?"

He leaned back and took out a cigarette.

"Sure, Doctor. When I look at my friends I'm acutely aware that I'm just not making it. They all drive better cars; they have bigger houses; they belong to the "in" country clubs; they make more money, and they have . . . they have . . ."

"They have *what*, Peter?"

Peter stammered.

"Uh, they have um . . . more exciting lives."

"You mean their extramarital sexual adventures?"

Peter squirmed in his seat.

"Uh, yeah, something like that. Hey, what are you smiling at, Doctor? What's so funny?"

"It's not really funny, Peter. I'm just thinking how much your friends must envy *you*. I'm sure they say, 'Hey, look at Pete! He's making money like crazy; he goes to Europe every year; he has that great-looking wife, and everything else anyone could want.' "

Peter brightened up.

"You really think so, Doctor?"

"I guarantee it. More than once I've had patients who are tremendously envious of a close friend—whom I happened to be treating at the same time. And guess what? The friend they envied so much was eaten up with envy of *them!*"

*E-n-v-y* is really shorthand for *e-n-e-m-y*. Dogging the footsteps of every human accomplishment is that terrible little inner voice that says, "Big deal! That's nothing compared with what someone else has acquired, accomplished, gained, bought . . ." One of the greatest enemies of happiness in this life is *envy*. If you stamp out envy, you will take a giant step forward toward lasting happiness.

Actually, envy can be divided into two major categories—material and emotional. In so-called modern society, which is just a fancy word for "industrial-materialistic" society, there is a constant external pressure to acquire material things. It's not just a car you need, but the ultimate in cars. A suit or a pair of shoes is not enough; you need the latest style in everything. What was "in" last year is "out" this year. There is the "in" neighborhood, the "in" country club, the "in" restaurants, and even the "in" cigarette—if you can believe *that!* You are trained to believe—just like Pavlov's dogs, by conditioned reflex—that you must constantly discard your current material possessions in favor of newer and more exciting ones.

Good luck! *There's no way to do it!* As soon as you conform to the latest style, it changes! Take the women's skirt sweepstakes, the men's tie sweepstakes, and the suit lapel sweepstakes. As soon as the men get outfitted with narrow lapels and narrow ties and the women are decked out in short skirts, some "taste maker" presses a button and the skirts have to slump, the ties have to sprawl, and the lapels have to expand. Anyone who doesn't instantly adjust their dimensions is made to feel like a social outcast. Silly? Superficial? Senseless? Of course! But it doesn't stop there.

You are constantly influenced by means of subtle and not-so-subtle mind-molding techniques to follow a precise pattern of behavior. You are constantly shown role models, on television, in magazines, in movies, in newspapers, that make you feel inferior and, above all, envious. The people you see are young, glamorous, wealthy, exciting, euphoric, and, above all, dripping with material possessions. Your tongue is supposed to hang out to your shoe tops when you see what *they* have and compare it with what *you* have. You are supposed to suffer intolerable pangs of envy. You are programmed to mortgage everything you have to acquire the latest plastic junk that will bring you up-to-date. Your intense suffering can be ended only by buying all the irresistible items that you are shown.

But, there are a couple of things you are *not* shown. First, you are *not* shown the fact that most of the people you see are actors and models—paid performers whose youth and exuberance are rented by the hour. When the camera clicks off they climb out of those fancy cars, slip off those elegant clothes, and hand over all that glittering jewelry. They put on their faded blue jeans, hoof it over to the subway, and ride home to their unfashionably dingy apartments. Furthermore, the "beautiful people" who are supposed to fill you with envy have the life expectancy of a mosquito. As soon as they begin to fade, they're finished, to be replaced by a new crop of younger and brighter professional pretties.

Of course, it's not all actors and models. Some of those super-rich and super-fashionable people out there are *real* people. They and their millions exist. Their cars are real. Their yachts are real. Their fancy clothes are real. That brings us to the second thing that you are *not* shown on television and in the movies. You are *not* shown the true disasters of the lives of the people who are supposed to make you envious. Oh, once in a while news of their drug addiction, their alcoholism, their disastrous personal lives floats to the surface like garbage on the surface of a pretty pond. That's when you see the emptiness of petty materialism. That's when it becomes crystal clear that the fanciest house in the world is not a substitute for real personal satisfaction and solid human values. That's when it should be obvious that a $75,000 sports car can't cuddle up to you at bedtime. That's when it should be obvious that you don't have *anything* to be envious of!

In societies based on ruthless competition, the constant struggle to be "best" doesn't end at the car dealer or the jewelry store. Once you have all that money can buy, you have to use it to acquire all that money *can't* buy. You have to get invited to the "right" parties, associate with the "right" people, and be the "right" kind of person yourself. You have to talk the "right" way. You have to walk the "right" way. You have to think the "right" way. But how do you do that? How do you get invited? How do you cultivate the "right" people? How do you make yourself desirable as a "right" person? Listen, as Ginny tells you the details.

A plain white blouse and a pale blue skirt—they were simple, tasteful, and perfect for setting off her long red hair and green eyes. But they didn't match what Ginny was saying:

"Oh, Doctor, it's so important to know the right people! I mean, there's so much they can do for one!"

"But you don't really believe that, do you, Ginny?"

Ginny burst out laughing.

"Of course not, Doctor! Don't be silly!"

Suddenly she became serious.

"But I once did. Not too long ago this kind of silliness was my whole life. Beautiful people, beautiful places, beautiful parties—I used to be proud of my lifestyle. You'll never believe the lengths I went to to be invited to a party. Thank goodness that's over."

"Why do you say that?"

"Because that's what opened my eyes. It was about a year ago, and it was the big party of the year in Palm Springs—of all places. There were going to be people from St. Tropez, Lugano, London! I can even remember how that used to impress me: 'Mr. and Mrs. John Jones, of Cleveland, Ohio and London.' Wow! Anyhow, Rhonda was the lady in question. She was kind of the 'Queen of the Social Scene' at that time. She decided—goodness knows how—who was socially acceptable and who wasn't, what was "in" and what was "out," and who was invited and who wasn't invited. Actually, she seemed to spend most of her time deciding whom *not* to invite."

Ginny shook her head.

"Anyhow it got down to about four days before the

party and I still hadn't gotten an invitation. My husband was a stockbroker and he was desperate to go—he said for business reasons but I know he just loved that scene. So I took the bull by the horns, and I went to see Rhonda one morning about ten. It was just what you'd expect: circular driveway, matched Dobermans, silver gray Rolls-Royce parked in front, and a house out of a movie set. A butler answered the door, I dropped my calling card on his little silver tray. You're surprised? Well, I was really into it in those days, Doctor.

"Anyhow, after I had waited about ten minutes in a tennis court-sized living room, the butler showed me into Rhonda's bedroom. I had my speech all ready: 'Rhonda, you may not remember me, but we met at General Crandon's ranch. You were with the Senator, and I was sort of just standing around. Well, anyway, there's something really important that I want to talk to you about. I mean, it may not be important to *you,* but . . .'"

Ginny paused.

"As I walked down the hallway rehearsing that awful boot-licking little speech, Doctor, my mouth was going dry and my heart was pounding. I was scared stiff. I was just turning the doorknob on Rhonda's bedroom door when I heard a funny little noise, like a metallic 'clunk!' I couldn't exactly place it but that 'clunk' was what saved my life—and restored my sanity.

"I walked into the bedroom and there was Rhonda, half-reclined on the bed—a sensational bed with what looked like a gigantic seashell for a headboard. The whole bedroom was some decorator's fantasy. It was white satin and black marble and—well, that doesn't matter now. Rhonda was so friendly I couldn't believe it! She said: 'Ginny, I'm so delighted to see you! Come right in!'

"I thought to myself: 'Well, Ginny, this is one party you're going to be invited to!'

"She said, 'Come on, sit over here on the bed with me!' That made me a little uneasy, if you know what I mean,

Doctor. But as I approached the bed I noticed that her face was a little flushed. As I turned the corner of the bed I saw it right there on the floor!''

''What was it?''

''It was a very expensive mirrored wastebasket, Doctor. And it was almost full of . . . of . . .''

''Of what, Ginny?''

Ginny burst out laughing.

''It was almost full of *beer cans!* Ten o'clock in the morning and the Queen of the Social Scene was getting loaded on *canned beer!* That was the 'clunk' I heard—the latest empty beer can falling on top of the rest! And it was the cheapest supermarket brand to boot! Doctor, I got out of there so fast I don't even remember getting in my car. And that morning I left any envy I ever had for the ''in'' group right there in that mirrored wastebasket—alongside all those cheap beer cans!''

Envy of someone else's lifestyle is based on ''misleading identifications.'' People who are naive and inexperienced think that imitating a person's manner of speaking, dressing, walking, and posing will make them like that person. Of course, it doesn't work that way. You can speak with an Oxford accent but that doesn't make you a graduate of Oxford. And even being a graduate of Oxford doesn't guarantee that you will be a happy and successful person. The goal of life is not to make yourself into a carbon copy of a carbon copy! The truth is that the very people who are knocking themselves out to impress you are the ones who are the most insecure and most desperate to be accepted by everyone else.

The ultimate solution to the problem of envy is to be yourself. Concentrate all your energy and all your ability on fulfilling your own potential. Remember, *you* are all you've got! And even more important, *you* are all you need! You don't *ever* have to envy anyone else.

# 13
# Female Orgasm

IN A REAL SENSE female orgasm is like the weather: Everybody talks about it, but hardly anybody does anything about it. Fortunately, that's where the comparison ends. You *can't* do anything about the weather, but a woman *can* do plenty about achieving an orgasm.

One of the big problems in dealing with the problem of orgasm in women is that no one knows what an orgasm really is. We know about the erection of the clitoris, the tightening of the vagina, the various secretions and all that. But that doesn't tell us why some women have orgasms with no trouble and why other women have trouble with orgasms. There even seems to be a lot of confusion about where the female orgasm occurs—in the clitoris or in the vagina. Let's see if we can clear up that confusion once and for all and in the process try to make it possible for every woman to have orgasms when and where she pleases.

We've all read those statistics which claim that only 50 percent or so of women reach orgasm. Well, don't you believe it. The truth is that 99.99 percent of women can reach orgasm—one way or another. *Almost every woman in the world can achieve a sexual climax by masturbation.*

That's probably the most important fact about female orgasm that exists. That establishes once and for all that orgasm occurs *neither* in the clitoris *nor* in the vagina. *The only place that orgasm occurs is in the brain!* Not only is that important but it's the key to making orgasm during intercourse available to virtually every woman.

If you think about it a moment, it has to be true. It's the only explanation for the fact that many women have orgasms while they are asleep. Even more interesting is that during brain surgery, stimulation of certain areas of the brain can produce an impressive orgasm. Those simple facts must revolutionize our thinking about orgasm. All a woman has to do to achieve dependable and satisfying orgasms once and for all is to change the way her brain reacts to sexuality. For most women who have orgasm problems, that means turning their thoughts back to childhood. That was the time when most of the mental roadblocks to orgasm were placed at strategic crossroads in their minds. Cynthia is going through it right now:

"You ask if I had a happy marriage, Doctor? Yes and no."

"Could you be a little more specific, Cynthia?"

Cynthia carefully smoothed some imaginary wrinkles out of her skirt and looked at me hesitatingly. With her alabaster white skin, long red hair, and pale blue eyes, she was very attractive.

"I'm sure you've heard this problem before. I'm twenty-four, I've been married a year, and I've had exactly three orgasms in that time. And you asked me if I was happily married?"

"I understand. Now let me ask you a few more questions to help me understand the situation better. Did you have orgasms during intercourse before you were married?"

Cynthia blushed to the roots of her carrot-red hair.

"I—I—well, you know . . ."

"Hold on a minute, Cynthia, let me explain. I'm asking you these questions as a doctor. I need to know what's happened in the past so I can help you in the present. Just relax and tell me what I need to know. Okay?''

Cynthia nodded.

''Fine. Well, that's the funny part. Jeff—that's my husband—and I lived together for about six months before we decided to get married, and during that time I had pretty regular orgasms. I'd say, about half the time when we had intercourse.''

''And by masturbation?''

Cynthia recoiled at the word.

''Sorry, Cynthia, but that's what they call it. Why does it bother you so much?''

''Because it always made me feel so guilty whenever I was doing it. You know, my mother never told me anything about sex or menstruation or anything like that. I guess you might say it was forbidden even to talk about it. I found out what little I knew from my girl friends, and they didn't know too much. I think of my teens as my 'Dark Ages.' ''

''But you masturbated during your 'Dark Ages?' ''

Cynthia blushed again—but less this time.

''Sure, I did. Even if I didn't have a normal sex education I still had normal feelings. But I really felt guilty about it.''

''And when you masturbate now, you don't have any trouble reaching an orgasm?''

''Of course not. I only wish I could get the same results with Jeff.''

''I think you'll be able to before long. Look. It's obvious that sex was a forbidden area when you were developing sexually. Like most teenage girls, you masturbated and enjoyed it and felt guilty about it. The problem is guilt and sexual satisfaction got linked together in your mind. Then when you lived with Jeff—before you got married— you had enough guilt to make the sexual satisfaction easy to come by. In a certain way, because sex outside of marriage impressed you as 'forbidden,' it made it more exciting. Is it clear so far?''

"Clear as crystal! Please go on.''

"Fine. Remember your mother wouldn't have approved of the way you were having sex before marriage. But after you were married, everything was 'legal.' There was nothing 'forbidden,' and there were hardly any orgasms. Let's look for another clue. How do you masturbate now?''

Cynthia blushed again—but just a tiny bit.

"In the shower. I let the stream of water run on my clitoris until I come. It's just the way I used to do it when I was in my teens.''

"Okay. So you can see what's happening. Your body—and your sexual organs—are in the present, but your sexual adjustment is about ten years behind. The way things are now you have two separate activities—orgasms and intercourse with your husband. If we can just bring the two activities together, then your problem will be solved.''

Cynthia smiled.

"I'd certainly like that, Doctor! What do I have to do?''

"Just keep listening, Cynthia. Since the brain is where all the sexual action really takes place, what we have to do is reprogram that organ so that it can reach an orgasm when and where you want it to. The sexual organs themselves—the clitoris and vagina—are simply receptors and transmitters. They receive physical sensations—touch and pressure and heat—and transmit them via the nerves to the brain. To reach an orgasm you have to have two things happening. First, you have to have a steady stream of sexual sensation arriving at the brain. Second, you have to have a brain that receives and stores those sensations and builds them up to the critical level. Then the brain has to let go and fire all that nervous energy off at once in a nice big orgasm. It also helps if the sexual stimulation starts gently and builds up to a crescendo.''

"But how do you know that for sure, Doctor?''

"It's obvious, Cynthia. That's what you do in the shower, isn't it?"

Cynthia thought for a moment.

"I guess you're right. Please go on."

"All right. Well, probably the first step in reprogramming the brain is to undo the old taboos. I'd guess your mother told you you shouldn't 'touch yourself down there.' "

Cynthia nodded vigorously.

"You bet she did!"

"Well, a good place to start might be 'touching yourself down there.' Find a quiet spot where you won't be interrupted, and lie down with a mirror and a good light. Check out your sexual organs once and for all. You'll notice some fascinating things."

Cynthia raised her pretty eyebrows.

"For example?"

"For example, notice how the little hood over the clitoris is attached to the smaller lips that cover the vagina. During intercourse, as the penis goes in and out, it pulls down on those little cables and massages the clitoris. Just let your curiosity loose and you'll discover some very interesting things."

She put her fingers to her lips.

"But Doctor! That would make me feel so funny. It's like perverted, looking at myself down there!"

"Of course, that's the problem, Cynthia. You look at your fingernails very carefully, and you polish them and you paint them and all that. That doesn't make you feel 'perverted,' does it?"

"No, but that's different!"

"It sure is. I'd say your sexual organs are a lot more important to your happiness than your fingernails.

Cynthia smiled.

"Well, when you put it that way, Doctor, I have to agee!"

"Fine. Let's see if you're ready for the next step."

Cynthia stiffened ever so slightly.

"Oh, Doctor, what's the next step?"

"Just what you've been doing for at least ten years—reaching an orgasm on your own. But this time I want you to observe it carefully so you can learn exactly what's going on. I think you'll notice some things that are especially interesting."

"Such as?"

"Well, you'll notice that you start off gently—barely touching yourself. As the blood begins to fill the clitoris and the lips of the vagina, you feel the need for stronger stimulation. That's what I was describing when I said that the impulses to the brain have to get faster and more intense. You'll also notice at the beginning you have complete conscious control. You can change technique or stop anytime. But as you proceed it's as if the brain is insisting on more and more stimulation and you begin to lose control of what you're doing. For example, you eventually reach the point where you have to keep rubbing your clitoris faster and faster, no matter what. That's very important."

"But why is it so important?"

"Because the sooner you lose control of yourself consciously, the more likely you are to have an orgasm."

"But that's hard, Doctor!"

"I know it's hard. All your life you've been told that you *must control yourself!* And you *have* been controlling yourself. That's why you haven't had many orgasms since you've been married. Now what you have to do is *let yourself go.* You have to pull down all the barriers to sexual enjoyment—those same barriers that you yourself erected according to the blueprint your mother supplied."

"That sounds like a hard job!"

"It is a hard job. But everyone who's done it agrees it's worth doing."

Cynthia smiled mischievously.

"I'll bet! But don't stop!"

"Okay. Every sexual experience—whether it's masturbation or intercourse—has to have a beginning, a middle, and an end. In reaching an orgasm the goal is to keep a constant stream of steadily increasing impulses reaching the brain from the vagina and clitoris until the critical point is reached and the orgasmic explosion occurs."

Cynthia raised her hand slightly.

"But, Doctor, I have a question. Is it just the clitoris and vagina that are involved?"

"Of course not, Cynthia, but that's where the main action is. You know what they say: 'All's fair in love and war.' Well, you can consider orgasm as part of the 'war for love.' So all's fair in orgasm as well. I'm sure you've noticed how squeezing and rubbing the nipples and breasts intensify the sensations that you feel during masturbation and intercourse. And there are a lot of other things you can do during sex to intensify those impulses that are flooding the brain."

Cynthia leaned forward slightly.

"Such as?"

"Well, the brain can process impulses from all five senses. So every type of feeling, if it's appropriate, can reinforce sexual excitement, help you give up conscious control, and make orgasm come faster and harder. Kissing, for example, includes touch, taste and smell. That's another important part of establishing orgasm—you have to give yourself every possible boost. For example, when you masturbate you do everything you can think of to reach a climax. It's only reasonable to do the same thing when you're having regular intercourse."

Cynthia paused, then spoke.

"Does that mean using your imagination too, Doctor?"

Sure, and it means using your imagination in two ways. First, it means using fantasy to reinforce the stimulation to the brain. You've used fantasy when you've masturbated, haven't you?"

Cynthia didn't answer but she nodded her head.

"And you can do the same thing during intercourse if it helps.

"You can also use your imagination in another way during intercourse."

Cynthia frowned.

"How's that, Doctor?"

"By thinking up new ways to fire those impulses up to the brain. For example, having your husband work on your clitoris until you reach an orgasm can be . . ."

Cynthia interrupted.

"But isn't the idea to have an orgasm by regular intercourse?"

"That's what I was just about to say."

"Oh, I'm sorry, Doctor. This is so important to me that I guess I'm just getting a little excited."

"That's all right, Cynthia, I understand. Anyway, if your husband can bring you to a climax that way, it's an important achievement. For some women it's the first time they have an orgasm with a partner. Sometimes they can go right from there to having an orgasm during intercourse."

"And if they can't?"

"That's where the imagination comes in. Some women find that cunnilingus—mouth-clitoris or mouth-vagina stimulation—moves them toward orgasm like nothing else. Again, they have their orgasms first that way, and then later on they use cunnilingus as a preliminary stimulation before having orgasm by intercourse."

Cynthia hesitated.

"What is it, Cynthia?"

"Uh, what about the other way? You know . . ."

"You mean what they call, in those medical words, 'fellatio' or mouth-penis stimulation?"

"Uhm, yes. That's what I was thinking."

"Sure. More women than you imagine find that exciting, and sometimes it's really helpful to move them toward orgasm. It seems to help them 'let go' sooner than they'd be able to otherwise."

It was about a month later when Cynthia stopped in to see me again.

"Well, how's it going, Cynthia?"

A smile from ear to ear.

"Fine, Doctor, just fine. It took me about three weeks of hard work. No, really, it *was* hard work."

"I didn't say anything, Cynthia. I know it was hard work."

"Well, you know. A lot of people might make fun of it, but a lot of times I had to just buckle down and tell myself that no matter how embarrassed I felt or how nervous I got I just had to do what I had to do. And I did it. After about the third week, one night when I least expected it, it just happened. And it was really sensational. You know, there's a big difference when you do it to yourself and when it happens with your husband. It's really a supersensational feeling! You know what I mean?"

"I know what you mean. But you're not through yet."

Cynthia's eyes widened.

"I'm not through yet? You mean there's more?"

"Yes, in a certain sense. Although your next assignment may not be too hard to take. Once you get to the point where you can reach an orgasm during intercourse, you have to keep reinforcing those new patterns to make sure they are firmly established. That means that you should have intercourse as frequently as you can and make sure you reach an orgasm as often as possible."

Cynthia smiled again.

"I'm glad to hear you say that, Doctor, because that's *exactly* what I intended to do!"

# 14
# Gambling

"GAMBLING!" Just the word is enough to stir excitement! It conjures up images of the Great Casino at Monte Carlo, of dashing gentlemen in tuxedos and ravishing ladies in French evening gowns. The roulette wheel whirs quietly, the croupier murmurs, *"Rien ne va plus!"* and fortunes are made and lost as the little ball drops into the tiny depression on the polished mahogany wheel.

*"Vingt-quatre rouge!"* "Twenty-four red!"

The croupier rakes a giant stack of chips off the table and slides them in front of a small dark man wearing an immaculate white turban. He reaches out to take the chips and . . .

Suddenly the television screen fills with a commercial for after-shave lotion. The grade-B spy movie will continue in sixty seconds.

Now to reality. An icily air-conditioned room about the size and shape of an abandoned stable is filled with stooped gray-haired men and women. Each one has a small plastic cup full of quarters. The room is jammed with slot machines, and robotlike, the men and women mechanically slide coins into slots and pull the levers. Barely waiting to see the result, they continue dropping coins they can't afford to lose into the dead mouths of the machines.

In an even larger and more depressing room next door, there are a dozen dice tables. Standing over one is a chubby accountant from Los Angeles. He cradles a pair of dice in his right hand. In his left hand he grips ten one-hundred-dollar chips. He raises his right hand to his lips and whispers to the two small plastic cubes: "Please! Pleeeease! Pleeeeeze! Come on! You got to do it for me!"

He drops the chips on the table, takes a long drink from a highball glass, and jerkily throws the dice. The small plastic cubes tumble over and over, slowed by the green felt. Suddenly they stop. On the upper surface of the one cube there are four white dots. The other cube has three tiny white specks showing. The total is seven. The accountant from Los Angeles loses—for the eleventh time in a row. His total loss for the evening is $4,450. His loss for the past three days is $29,670. He shakes his head, takes the elevator up to his room, and swallows thirty-one sleeping tablets. That was two weeks ago. Today he sits in my office.

"I knew it was wrong just as soon as I swallowed them, Doctor. I called the desk right away. They got an ambulance. In the hospital they pumped my stomach—boy, was that awful! And then the management bought me a plane ticket home. But you know, while they were pumping my stomach, there was one thought that kept going through my head.

"What was that, Harold?"

Harold grinned mischievously.

"I kept thinking, 'These casinos took me for everything I had, and now they're even trying to take back the drinks they gave me!' "

Harold suddenly became serious.

"I know it's nothing to laugh about, Doctor. I'm just glad it was my own money I lost. I know one man in my position who lost company money. He's in Brazil now."

"A fugitive?"

"No, he's a missionary. He paid the money back, got probation, and decided to become a missionary. It was about the only thing he could do after his wife left him, and of course, he couldn't get a job anywhere. Well, that's his problem. I'm here to talk about mine. The question that bothers me the most is, 'Why do I still find gambling so fascinating?' Can you answer that question for me?"

"Maybe. Maybe we can find a hint in one little fact about gambling that most people don't pay much attention to."

"What's that, Doctor?"

"It's the fact that the people who own the casinos never gamble. You never see one of those heavyweights out in Las Vegas hunched over the crap tables sweating blood and watching their life savings melt away. Do you know why?"

Harold smiled faintly.

"Keep going, Doctor, you're doing fine."

"Because, Harold, they know the secret. And that's exactly the secret I'm going to tell you right now. The secret is there's no such thing as gambling!"

"What do you mean? What have I been doing for the past nine years? If it wasn't gambling, what was it that took about one hundred and fifty thousand dollars of my life savings?"

"Well, it wasn't gambling, Harold, but we'll get to that later. But think about it. Those fellows who own the games don't take any risks. They're in business to win, no matter what. The poor suckers who bet are betting against a machine—a machine they can't see and they can't feel, but it's a machine just the same. Want me to tell you the name of it?"

"Keep right on going, you're doing fine."

"The name of that machine is the *Law of Probability*. All those casino owners have to do is fill their places with players—the Law of Probability does the rest. That's why they have all the shows with the naked girls and the big swimming pools and free drinks and cheap food. They just have to keep feeding suckers into that machine!''

Harold was listening intently now.

''The problem is that most people don't understand how the Law of Probability works. Basically, it operates like this: If you take a coin and flip it in the air, half the time it will come up heads and half the time it will come up tails. That is, if you throw it with about the same force and the same spin each time. It may come up heads ten times in a row, but then sooner or later it will have to come up tails ten times in a row to even things out. It's not *exactly* that way, but it's reasonably close. Now let's analyze roulette. You can play it many different ways, but imagine that you're just betting on the colors—*red* or *black*. It really sounds easy. You stay there and play all night, drink the free drinks, and if the Law of Probability works—and it *always* works—you come out even. In the long run, red comes up half the time and black comes up half the time. So you just bet one color, and you can't lose. You can't win, but you're home free. Half the time you're right and half the time you're wrong. A nice evening and it doesn't cost you a thing. Right?''

Harold thought for a moment.

''It sounds reasonable.''

He scratched his head.

''What is it, Harold?''

''Well, if you can do it that way, where do they get the millions of dollars to build all those fancy casinos? And where do the casino owners get their Mercedes and Rolls-Royces? Not from the guys that play one color all night and never lose a dollar.''

''Right you are, Harold! They have to depend on high rollers like you. But they don't even let the dollar-chip players win at roulette. And remember, ordinarily the best odds you can get are playing the red or black in roulette.''

''Then how does it work?''

''Like this. There are thirty-six numbers—plus a zero

and a double zero. Every time that wheel spins, it can come up red, black, zero, or double zero. If you always play the red, you lose on black, zero, or double zero. (In European casinos they only have one zero, but it's enough to put you away all by itself.) That's it, Harold. That's all it takes to build those big hotels, equip those fancy casinos, and pay for a new Rolls-Royce every year. Those two zeros tilt the odds against you just enough so that you can never come out ahead. They adjust that gigantic cosmic machine called the Law of Probability to carefully grind you into a fine white powder. If you play long enough, *you have to lose*."

"How about the other games?"

"They're only about ten times worse. Roulette, depending on how you figure it, is about 1.1 to 1 against you. That's guaranteed to wipe you out. The other games range from the impossible to the ridiculous. Take the slot machines. A very *generous* payoff is forty percent of the amount that comes in. A lot of machines only return thirty percent. But even with a forty percent payoff, you are absolutely destroyed. When you branch out into the dice tables and blackjack, you can just about forget it.

Harold looked indignant.

"But I've read about all those people who win big in the casinos!"

"I bet you have! Casinos all around the world are very good at public relations. When a customer *wins* big, it gets all over the newspapers. When a customer *loses* big and takes an overdose of sleeping pills, where do you read about it? I know about the 'card counters' at Blackjack too. Those are the folks who memorize the cards so they know when the picture cards are coming up and when they're not. The casinos complain a lot about them, but I get the feeling that they're not suffering too much. Besides, they have their own methods for dealing with players who try to beat the system. Again one of the problems you have, Harold, is that you don't gamble."

Harold's mouth fell open.

"I don't gamble? What are you talking about? Can't you see my scars?

I couldn't help chuckling.

"Sure, I can, Harold. But those scars aren't from gambling. They're from throwing your money away with both hands. Gambling means betting on something where the outcome is not certain and only subject to the laws of chance. For example, if you bet even money as to which of two crows sitting on a fence will fly off first, that *might* be gambling. But if you bet that a little ball won't land on zero or double zero or if you bet on which piece of colored paper will come off the top of a pile of colored papers called 'playing cards,' that's not gambling. If you bet against impossible odds about which dots will come up on some dice, that's not gambling. That's being slaughtered."

Harold thought for a moment.

"What about the lottery? That's a random event that no one can influence, isn't it? That's real gambling!"

"Hardly. Remember the odds have to be at least even. For every dollar you bet you get another dollar back if you win. And to be really fair, there have to be only two possible winners—you or someone else. The odds against winning on the lottery are so great—all the way from a hundred to one against you to a million to one against you—that it's not really gambling. It's just wishing. The sad truth is that casinos are not operated as places to gamble."

"Then what are they?"

"*Dream parlors*, Harold. They are *dream parlors*."

"What does that mean?"

"Simply this. A casino is a place where you can go and see a lot of money. There's at least a million dollars or so floating around at any given moment. They have pretty colors and dim lights and beautiful girls and free liquor and plush carpets and everything designed to put you into a kind of dream state. Then they offer you the *illusion* of taking some of that money for yourself. All you have to do is find the magic combination. If you can pick the magic number or the card or the throw of the dice, you can suddenly become rich. But the tragedy is you can't. There is a sound mathematical basis for every gambling game, and those numbers work against you. The men who own casinos are extremely sophisticated investors who hire the best mathematicians to design the games to guarantee that they *don't* lose. And incidentally to guarantee that you *do* lose. That's what the business is all about. It's the Big Claw all over again.''

"The Big Claw? What's the Big Claw?''

"Don't you remember, Harold? In the old penny arcades they used to have a big glass case full of nice shiny merchandise. There were things like big cigarette lighters and beautiful cigarette cases. Then there were cases full of nice jewelry—heavy rings and bracelets. They were all shiny and gold-plated. The kids put their nickels in, and a big claw, like on a crane for a construction project, reached down and scooped up four or five cigarette lighters or bracelets. It carried them over to the chute that would deliver them into their hands. Then just as the claw was about to open and drop all the booty into their waiting arms, the big claw moved a fraction of an inch and dropped its precious cargo back onto the pile of gleaming merchandise sitting there in the glass case. It never gave them a thing! And they knew it! But the hope, the temptation, the dream were so great that they dropped plenty of nickels into the slot. They always hoped somehow that something would go wrong with the system—that it would suddenly turn against its masters and fill their sweaty little hands with gleaming goodies.

Harold was smiling.

"I remember that, Doctor! I know what you mean.''

"I hope so, Harold. You and all the other so-called gamblers are just dream junkies. You hang out in the dream parlors letting your fantasies roll and paying the price. When the dream is over you don't win anything and you lose what you had to begin with. That's when you have to face reality and that's when you popped your sleeping pills."

"Wow! That sure makes sense, Doc! Is that all there is to it?"

"Not quite. A lot of the people who call themselves gamblers really want to lose. I remember one patient of mine who 'got lucky' one night and won ten thousand dollars at the dice tables. Gamblers say 'got lucky,' but that's not really what happens. What happens is that they come into a game at a particular part of a mathematical cycle. That is, they may start playing the black in roulette when black is coming up four or five or fifteen times in a row. For mathematicians, that's nothing unusual. But black then has to lose the same number of times. So if you get in the 'winning' part of a cycle, you call yourself 'lucky.' Then if you get out before the cycle switches, you keep your money. That's what happened to this patient of mine."

Harold spoke eagerly.

"Then there *are* some winners?"

"Judge for yourself. He cashed in his chips, took one hundred hundred-dollar bills upstairs to his room with him, and went to bed. It was about ten at night. Even though he'd been at the dice tables since about ten that morning, he absolutely could *not* fall asleep. He tossed and turned, wiggled and twitched, for the next five hours. Finally he got up, got dressed, took his ten thousand dollars, and went down to the casino again. He started shooting dice, and in an hour he'd lost every penny. Then he went up to his room, went to bed, and slept like a baby."

Harold was shaking his head.

"I know the feeling, Doctor! I know the feeling! I guess it's kind of dumb to let your future depend on which hole in a wooden wheel a little steel ball drops into."

"You're right, Harold. Another patient once said to me: 'I'm tired of lending a lot of money to a pair of dice—and the dice take the money and never pay it back!' I think that sums it up pretty well. Do you agree?"

"You can bet on it!"

Harold grinned.

"No, that's not the way I want to say it anymore. Let me just say, I agree one hundred percent."

Of course, all the gambling isn't done in the casinos. Remember the saying "The gambling called *'Business'* looks with cold disapproval on the business called *'Gambling.'* "

A great deal of what passes for "investments" and "business" is really thinly disguised gambling. Take the stock market, for example. The trappings are different from the main room of a casino, but you find a lot of the same dream-parlor atmosphere. The computer displays flicker constantly, telephones jangle furiously, the stockbrokers jabber excitedly. Hundreds of millions of dollars change hands every minute. There is tension in the air. And there is something else in the air—the hope, the wish, the *illusion* of cheating destiny and getting rich.

Of course, some people do get rich in the stock market. Remember the story of the man from Cleveland who visited a stockbroker friend in New York City? The friend took the visitor on a tour of the stock exchange, the brokers' offices, and the vast computer networks operating behind the scenes. It was a nice summer day, and afterward the broker took the visitor down the street to the yacht harbor. He pointed at fifteen or twenty beautiful vessels at anchor offshore and proudly announced: "There are the stockbrokers' yachts!"

The visitor looked in awe, thought a moment, and then said: "How nice! But where are the *customers'* yachts?"

Of course, that's the question. So often what people like to call an "investment" in the stock market is no more than a heavy bet on the big computerized roulette wheel. Who knows whether the common stock of General Motors or U.S. Steel or Xerox or General Mills or any other of the thousands of stocks traded every day will go up or down or sideways? More interesting, 99 percent of the gamblers—pardon me, investors—make their choices on the basis of hunches, wishful thinking, or advice from "experts." Incidentally, there's something fascinating about that expert advice. It gives almost exactly the same results as the roulette wheel: If you stay with it long enough, you lose everything.

Who really knows whether a stock is going to go up or down? The officers of the company know. And according to U.S. federal law they can't tell you. (It's called "insider information.") So anyone else who gives advice, *according to law, is only guessing*. That's worth thinking about.

Another form of gambling that masquerades as "investment" is the futures market. That's where you buy the obligation to buy or sell a commodity such as wheat, corn, gold, copper, and so on at some future time. That can really make your toes tingle because the amounts are immense. For example, if you start to play in that league, you deal in terms of five thousand bushels of wheat or twenty-five thousand pounds of copper or ten tons of cocoa. To make matters more interesting you have to put down only a small deposit—sometimes as little as 5 percent of the value. In the casino that would be called gambling on credit. If you bet on a commodity to go up and it goes down fast, you can lose a hundred thousand dollars in a single day. That's real action! And of course, if you guess right, you can make a lot of money. For some reason, not too many people guess right. Most people who play the commodities markets don't have any more idea what will happen to them than they do in the casinos. It's the old dream parlor at work again.

Okay, what's the solution to gambling? Well, there's

only one. If you really like to gamble, look for two crows sitting on a fence. At least those birdies will give you an even chance. But all those other games—blackjack, dice, roulette, and the rest—those are just ways to sell you dreams, and very expensive dreams at that. If you want to win, there's only one way to do it—don't gamble.

## 15
## Hard Drugs

OKAY, SO YOU THINK you're hooked on hard drugs? Well, before we go any further let's make sure we agree on what a *hard drug* really is. By *traditional medical* definition a *hard drug* is one that causes actual physical dependence. That means the drug becomes part of your body metabolism and your body doesn't function adequately without the drug. The example that you will read about in all the official textbooks is the opium family: *morphine, opium, heroin*, and the rest. As you can imagine, it isn't quite that easy, but we'll come to that in a little while.

A more intelligent and useful way to define a *hard drug* is one that drastically changes how you think or behave—a drug that really zaps your brain once you get on it. Here's a sample list; there are plenty more in that category, of course: *cocaine, LSD, mescaline, amphetamines, barbiturates, quaaludes (ludes)*, and *alcohol*.

I know that cocaine isn't physically addicting, but I also know that it triggers dramatic behavior changes—so for purposes of dealing with this problem, it's a *hard drug*. Alcohol is a special problem that we've already discussed in a separate chapter.

114

Okay, let's start with the worst possible situation first—just to show you that the problem isn't as desperate as it may seem. Doctors, law-enforcement people, concerned family, and similar folks sometimes get a little hysterical about the subject of drugs—any drugs. But when it comes to hard drugs they can really get carried away. So with that in mind, let's start with heroin. Heroin is a derivative of opium that is a super analgesic. It relieves pain dramatically and also makes you feel good—happy, cheerful, and optimistic. That's why a puritanical medical profession refuses to use it as a medical drug in the United States. You are allowed to have something for pain, but you're not allowed to have something that relieves the pain *and* makes you feel good. (Heroin is used in other countries as a medical drug with excellent results.) This whole hard-drug business is full of oddities. The big thing in the United States these days is the use of methadone, an opium derivative, as a *treatment* for heroin addiction. The idea is to take the patient off heroin by giving him or her progressively smaller doses of methadone. Methadone is just as addicting as the rest of the opium group. U.S. doctors like it because it doesn't make you feel happy, like heroin does. Interesting?

Heroin, morphine, methadone, and the rest of the opium family are truly addicting in that they become part of the body's chemical reactions and when you stop taking them, things go haywire *for a while*. But it isn't all that bad. Typically it takes about a week to overcome the *physical* dependency on opium derivatives. The withdrawal reaction is really like a superhangover, with the user suffering from nausea, vomiting, diarrhea, anxiety, and assorted aches and pains. Thousands of people have quit cold turkey. They just grit their teeth and sweat it out; they seem to be none the worse for wear. There's another encouraging note. Most of the heroin and similar drugs that are sold illegally are tremendously watered down so that the average "drug addict" isn't nearly as hooked as he or she may believe. That makes the withdrawal syndrome much milder than most people have been led to expect.

Of course, it's better to come down from an opium drug under medical supervision. A good doctor can alleviate about 90 percent of the suffering during that crucial week. Once you're past that hurdle, there is no further *physical craving* for the drug. Read that again, please. The key word is *"physical."* What made you—or someone you know—start on heroin or any of its relatives was *not* the physical need for heroin. It was—obviously—the *emotional necessity to zap your mind.* The truth is *the uncomfortable week that it takes to free yourself from the physical habit is the easiest part.* After that comes the real challenge: overcoming the *emotional* problems that made hard drugs seem like a good idea. This is a chapter on drugs—not on the underlying emotional problems—so we'll have to leave the details on relief from the specific emotional problems for another section. Of course, we will make some general observations as we go along.

Okay, let's summarize. If you or someone you care about is addicted to opium derivatives—heroin, methadone, meperidine, morphine, opium itself, or any of the others—keep this in mind: The withdrawal reaction isn't as bad as they show it in the movies, and it's an essential first step to straightening out your life. Don't misuse fear of the withdrawal syndrome as an alibi to keep using the drug.

That advice goes double for all the rest of the *non*-habit-forming hard drugs. The first and most important step is to get off them—promptly and completely. Why? Because they are mind drugs—by definition. They impair the way your mind works, and they keep you from ever getting your thoughts together to the point where you can deal with your underlying problems. So, the first step is to *stop.* Now let's get to some specifics.

If you're hooked on amphetamines, you can stop cold without any serious danger *but* you want to do it under close medical supervision—perhaps in a hospital setting.

When it comes to downers—barbiturates, ludes, and the rest of the mind depressants—the key step is the same: get away from the pills. If you have a big bad habit, you just might have produced a *physical* dependency. In that rare case there can be a mini–withdrawal syndrome that lasts a couple of days or so. Again with the help of an experienced and sympathetic doctor, you can come through it relatively painlessly. But don't put it off: Start to stop as soon as you possibly can.

The hallucinogenic drugs—LSD, psilocybin, mescaline, and the rest—are rather bad news because they can do *permanent* damage to your brain, and fast. The best approach is *never* to take them at all or if you have taken them, *never* to try them again. After years of study and experience, we really know how much they clobber your brain. *No one with any sense fools around with hallucinogens.* They produce monster problems that no one really needs. Don't mess with them.

And now we come to cocaine. Until recently, cocaine was the favorite drug of the dregs of society. Prostitutes, petty criminals, mental defectives—they all sniffed cocaine to enable them to endure the daily tragedies of their lives. You had to be the last drip from the faucet of humanity to resort to those ugly white crystals. But now all that has changed. By a twist of fate—and clever publicity—cocaine is the darling of high society. Sniffed from the corner of a hundred-dollar bill, it is an affectation of the "beautiful people" at many discotheques and parties. Movie stars, sports stars, political stars, stars of all sizes and shapes use cocaine these days. How come? Well, they do it for about the same reason that prostitutes and petty thieves did it fifty years ago: *Cocaine is one of the most powerful antidepressant drugs known.*

Life is hard these days—probably harder than it has been for the past hundred years or so. After going through the familiar ritual of tranquilizers and antidepressant prescription drugs, some people continue to be depressed.

Often the ones who have the deepest and blackest depressions are the overachievers—the not-so-beautiful "beautiful people" and the superstars of our society. In the same group of cocaine users you can also find those halfway up or halfway down who would like to be at the top. For them, cocaine is the only way they can keep in there day after day.

From a medical point of view, cocaine does not produce physical dependency nor does it produce tolerance. There is no real withdrawal syndrome, and the dose that gives you a buzz today will give you more or less the same buzz tomorrow. (In contrast, opium drugs and amphetamines produce tolerance; users must gradually increase the dose to get the same effect.) But cocaine does have some big, big disadvantages. Aside from the expense, it does constant although gradual damage to the lining of your nose. Maybe that's not a problem right now, but five years from now you might still want to use your nose to breathe through. Cocaine can also produce bad brain changes such as paranoia and hallucinations, but in all honesty usually only when you take it intravenously. (Actually it's hard to imagine who would want to do something like that with such a potent drug, but as you may have noticed, people do all kinds of strange things.)

The worst part about using cocaine is the underlying reason that people use it: They can't come to grips with their real-life problems. If you're depressed, if you have obstacles in your path, if you feel defeated and desperate, cocaine makes all that disappear with one little sniff through one little nostril. Unfortunately, a few sniffs later, the cocaine is gone, and the problem is still there. Oh yes, there's one more little problem: Each sniff can set you back fifty or a hundred dollars.

That's the real defect with hard drugs. Not only do they not solve your problems, but they don't even allow you to escape them for more than a few scattered minutes during the day. Getting plugged into any hard drug is like driving as fast as you can to get to the gas station before you run out of gas. You know, and I know, and we all know—you just aren't going to make it!

So, if you're hooked on hard drugs, or somebody you care about is hooked on them, there's only one way out: *stop!* Stop as quickly and as completely as possible. Don't fall back on the transparent excuse that the withdrawal syndrome is so terrible. With the exception of the opiates, the withdrawal isn't that awful and you're going to have to do it anyway so you might as well get it over with. Even the opiate withdrawal isn't that bad with modern psychotropic drugs to help you through. Also, you may be pleasantly surprised to find that your habit isn't as big as you thought it was!

Oh yes, one other point. I hope nobody still believes the fairy tale about getting hooked on narcotics while getting morphine injections in the hospital after surgery. Every day millions of people get injections of morphine for pain without becoming addicted. (As we mentioned, in Great Britain, doctors may even give patients heroin.) Not one percent of one percent of hard-drug users get that way because of something they got from their doctors. The basic reason for using hard drugs is an underlying emotional problem. Because hard drugs are brain-altering drugs, the first step has to be *to stop the drug and allow the brain to recover physically*. Obviously, it's senseless to try to treat a brain that is drastically altered by the effects of the drug. The second step is, of course, to launch a vigorous attack against the underlying emotional problem. That makes drug use, from that moment on, senseless and irrelevant.

When's the best time to stop taking a hard drug? Well, what about right now, for instance? How about it?

# 16
# Impotence

IMPOTENCE. The word sends chills down the spine of every red-blooded man. It conjures up images of a flabby, pale, weak, trembling male totally unable to function sexually. *In reality, nothing could be further from the truth.* These are the facts:

1. There is no man on earth who has not suffered from impotence at some moment in his life.
2. The male sexual function is so unbelievably complex that sometimes it is a miracle that it even functions at all.
3. All of the mechanisms of the human mind and body are directed toward preventing and curing impotence. All we have to do is give them a chance to work.

With that in mind, let's move on to some important details. First of all there are some men who think they are impotent and who maybe aren't that way at all. See what you think about the following examples:

JOHN: I tell you, Doctor, it's really getting me down. I mean, I get an erection all right, but it just doesn't get hard enough. It's sort of half and half. It's enough to have intercourse with, but it just isn't the way I'd like it to be.

CHUCK: My problem is that I don't feel enough. When I ejaculate it's kind of halfhearted. I mean, it's not the big bang I was expecting.

NEIL: The first time it's all right, but when I try and do it again—say an hour later—I just can't get it up. What's going on?

I can see you smiling—and you're right. Neither John nor Chuck nor Neil suffers from impotence. They have other problems—more or less minor ones—but they are sexually potent. *Impotence is the inability to deliver a penis that's hard enough to go up into the vagina*. Understanding that immediately makes the problem much easier to solve. You don't need to get an erection like an iron lamp post to consider yourself potent. Something near the rigidity of a garden hose is more than adequate. (Unfortunately, a wet noodle will not do.) *But the truth is that 99 percent of men of any age are capable of making their penis hard enough to have normal intercourse*. How do they accomplish it? Hang on—that's where we're going. Before we proceed let's take a moment to understand what erection is all about.

In the human male the penis has a couple of long thin cylindrical sponges running along each side from the base almost to the tip. Normally, these sponges are dry and the penis hangs down in its normal position. But under certain well-known circumstances, tiny valves are opened within adjacent blood vessels and these sponges are flooded with blood. It's very similar to pumping up an air mattress except that the chambers are filled with blood instead of air. That makes the penis stand up at attention so that it can do what it's designed to do.

The process is a little more complicated than it seems since the blood has to be pumped into the sponges, the pressure has to be constantly monitored, and the valves have to be maintained in their closed positions. If things don't go just right, the blood drains from the chambers and the penis suddenly drops to half mast—or less. Now what controls all that pumping and filling and all the rest? You know what controls it—six pounds of very complicated jelly that sits on the end of your neck. Erection is directly under the control of the human brain. If the brain works right, the penis works right. If the brain slips up, the penis slips down. Here's a perfect example in the case of Dennis:

"You know, there's no reason in the world why this should be happening to me, Doctor."

Dennis wiped the sweat from his forehead with an immaculate white handkerchief. The creases in his pants were razor sharp, his shirt collar was carefully starched, and his shoes were polished to a brilliant gleam. He looked as if he had just stepped off the page of a men's fashion magazine.

"What do you mean by *this*, Dennis?"

Dennis winced just a little.

"Well, it's hard to talk about but I guess I might as well. It's this šex problem I have—I suppose you'd call it impotency. I mean, I just can't do it. It gets half-hard to begin with and then when I go to . . . you know . . . when I start to . . ."

"Put it in?"

"Yeah, put it in. I suppose it shouldn't be so hard to say it, but it's embarrassing. You know, I get all worked up and ready to go, but my erection just doesn't come."

"How does your wife react to that, Dennis?"

Dennis winced again.

"Funny you should ask, Doctor. That's the bad part. She just kind of purses her lips and rolls over and goes to sleep. She gives me a kind of disgusted look and usually doesn't even say anything."

"How does that make you feel?"

"Well, not too awfully good. Sort of guilty, like the whole thing's my fault and I ought to be able to do something about it on my own."

"And, of course, you can't."

"Of course, I can't. How can any man cure this problem himself? It takes two people to have sex."

"You're right. How would you describe your wife, Dennis?"

He thought a moment.

"Hmmm. Well, she's Swiss and very neat. Look at my shirt and my shoes. She actually shines my shoes herself!"

"How does she run the house?"

Dennis came up with half a grin.

"Like a Swiss watch. Everything has to work just right. The meals are on time—to the minute. The laundry gets done at the same hour every afternoon. Our house is a modern miracle of efficiency!"

"Except in the bedroom?"

Dennis nodded his head.

"Except in the bedroom."

"When did it start? I mean the drop-off in efficiency in the bedroom—in your sexual performance?"

Dennis frowned.

"How could I ever forget? It was about six months ago. We'd been out late to a party. I'm in the import business, and I always have clients visiting me from Europe. My wife sometimes goes along to help with the translation. We were at this nightclub, and they had a pretty daring show—you know, like some of the revues they have in Paris. I guess my wife must have gotten pretty turned on by some of what she saw."

"And when you got home?"

Dennis smiled—for the first time since he arrived in the office.

"There's nothing wrong with that, is there Doctor?"

"No, Dennis, there's probably something right with it. But go on."

"Anyhow, that night she wanted sex like almost never before. I have to say that my wife has always been kind of reserved when it came to sex, but that night something must have clicked because she was really turned on!"

"And her husband?"

Dennis shook his head.

"I still don't know what happened to me. I did have quite a bit to drink and I was worried about those clients. They were a tough bunch of Dutchmen who had threatened to cancel out. Anyhow, my wife was like a tigress and . . . and . . ."

"And you couldn't get an erection?"

"Not exactly. I got one—and a good one. Well, with what she was doing to me I couldn't help but get one. But as soon as I tried to put it in, it collapsed. I mean, it just died."

"And your wife?"

"She didn't actually say anything. She just pulled away from me and gave me a look of such hatred and contempt I can still see it. Every time we go to bed I can still see that look on her face! And if I have trouble—you know what I mean—she gives me that same look all over again."

"Does she ever say anything?"

"Sure. She says helpful little things like 'Why can't you do it anymore?' or 'Do you have another woman?' "

"Do you have another woman?"

Dennis turned red—bright red.

"I think you have to tell me everything if you want me to be able to help you."

"Sure. I know. Of course, I've had other women. Wouldn't I have been an idiot if I hadn't tried it with someone else just to see if it were really broken? Sure, I've had sex with other women."

"And?"

"Well, you must know the answer to that one. With other women everything is fine. But I know why."

"Why?"

"Because there's no pressure. It doesn't matter if I get an erection or not—so I do. But I want to have sex with my own wife in my own bedroom—not with some chick in a motel room somewhere."

Dennis was right—in more ways than one. And his experience with impotence is typical of what most men experience. The first failure can be for any one of a thousand reasons. You can list them alphabetically: alcohol, anger, anxiety, apprehension, and 996 reasons more. The male sexual reflexes are delicate, and it doesn't take much to throw them out of whack. But the first failure leads to the next one, and then the chain reaction is under way. Or as they say, impotence begins the first time you can't do it the second time and gets worse the second time you can't do it the first time.

Dennis's wife was a stickler for efficiency, and she couldn't accept the fact that his penis wouldn't work as dependably as her washing machine. Every time they had sex he ran the risk of her disapproval, and that was a risk he was afraid to run. His penis finally just decided not to try.

With other women it was different. He didn't really care what they thought about him, there was no risk, and so there was no impotence. Dennis's experience gives us a panoramic view of impotence and opens the door to solving the problem once and for all. And the place to start is with the most important male sex organ—the brain.

The first step in the chain of events that produces erection is psychological stimulation of the brain. That can be transmitted through any of the five senses—the sight of a beautiful woman, the smell of perfume that stirs memories of sex, the taste of a kiss, the sound of a woman's voice, the touch of a woman's hand. Any of these can trigger the nervous impulses that open the floodgates of the penis and produce a full-blown erection. If they all operate together, the erection they produce is likely to be harder, faster, and more intense.

Sometimes—as every man can testify—sexy thoughts are enough. There doesn't even have to be any physical stimulation—at least at first. However to *maintain* the erection there *must* be physical stimulation. That stimula-

tion can come from a woman's hand or mouth or vagina—
but it must come. Those are the positive elements of
producing and maintaining an erection. There are also
negative ones.

Sex is important—no denying that. But survival is even
more important. It's so important that any event which
causes fear or anxiety immediately scuttles sex and pre-
pares the man for fight or flight. (After all, how fast can
you run with a big hard erection?) A loud knock on the
door, a scream of fear from the woman, the sound of
someone else in the room, *the sudden memory of a frightening experience*—these are all enough to snap open the
valves and instantly drain the blood from the penis. *In
actual fact, sexual potency is a battle between the factors
that produce sexual stimulation and the ones that cancel
it.* So to cure—or prevent—impotence all we have to do is
suppress all the factors that work *against* sexual stimulation
and reinforce all the factors that *produce* sexual stimulation.
Of course, that's a complicated and time-consuming task,
but it's worth the effort. Here we go.

1. *The greatest enemy of sexual potency is society.* From
earliest childhood almost every man is told that sex is *bad*,
and modern society goes to great lengths to suppress sexual stimulation except, of course, to sell absolutely essential products like toothpaste, ball-point pens, panty hose,
and whiskey. The first lesson every man with a potency
problem has to learn is that sex is good, normal, human,
and desirable.

2. *Good health means good sex.* The number one sexual
organ—the brain—is a delicate and sensitive organ. It
responds badly to poisons and responds well to healthful
measures. If you want to recover from impotence (or
prevent it), the first thing to do is stop smoking and stop
drinking and stop taking drugs. That even includes prescription drugs since some of the most innocent-sounding
drugs have a way of walloping potency. If you absolutely

have to take a drug to keep alive, okay. But otherwise talk to your doctor about discontinuing it. And of course no doctor will prescribe drinking or smoking or marihuana or cocaine or any of the rest of the ''mind'' drugs. Those chemicals undermine sexuality in every way. (Sorry, but that's the way it is.)

The next step is to do everything possible to improve your physical health. Remember your brain and your nervous system are part of your body and if your body is physically sick, your brain is sick too. Good fresh natural foods, fresh clean air, and moderate and healthful exercise are simple and essential measures.

3. *You need someone fighting on your side.* Impotence is a tough problem in the sense that it takes a lot of good things happening at once to produce an erection but only one bad thing to kill an erection. *You need an eager and willing partner.* Your wife or girl friend has to be willing to do everything she can possibly do to increase the sexual stimulation to a maximum and to eliminate all antisexual influences. Unless she understands that, there is almost no chance of overcoming impotence with her. If she does understand it—and does everything possible to help you— you have every chance in the world of regaining your potency and keeping it.

4. *All's fair in the war for love . . . and potency.* The challenge is to flood the brain with enough sexual stimulation to overcome all the negative impulses—both past and present. That justifies taking almost any reasonable measure to increase sexual excitement. If having sex in a particular position or in a special setting is what turns you on, do it. If oral sex is what seems to do the trick, do it. If you are stimulated by pictures of ladies before they put their clothes on, that's all right too. You're fighting for your sexual survival—life without sex is *not* an exciting prospect for most men.

Of course, there are some limits. If you need to be strapped to a board and beaten with tire chains to get an erection, there is perhaps a little emotional conflict that you should work through first. But don't be afraid to take advantage of the routine repertoire of sexual fun and games to increase the positive impulses flowing through your nervous system.

5. *Success breeds success*. Once your potency is restored, keep at it. In sex, like in no other area, the rule is "Use it or lose it." Successful and satisfying intercourse reinforces the sexual reflexes and makes future sexual failures less and less likely. Within reason, the more often you can have sex, the better off you will be. To put it succinctly, successful sex is the best defense against impotence.

So, remember that impotence is *not* an incurable disease. It is not even a disease—just an imbalance of positive and negative sexual impulses reaching the brain. If you simply do everything you can to accentuate the positive impulses and shut off the negative impulses, you should have the problem licked.

# 17
# Insomnia

"I CAN'T SLEEP!"
  "I stayed awake all night!"
  "I hardly sleep at all anymore!"
  "I didn't close my eyes for one second last night!"

Have *you* ever said things like that? Sure you have, because from time to time everyone in this world has some little difficulty falling asleep. Most of the time we make it up the next night—or sometimes even the next day. But there are moments when sleep just won't come. There are times in everyone's life when no matter how hard you try, you just can't sleep. That's what this chapter deals with.

Before we really get into it, let's take a look at what sleep is really all about. The human brain is in constant intense activity during three-quarters of each day. In order to restore itself and function efficiently, it needs to rest about one-quarter of the time. We call that rest period "sleep." Obviously, the brain doesn't shut off during that time because it has some very important "housekeeping" functions to attend to. It has to supervise the beating of the heart, the breathing and respiration, the operation of the kidneys, and all the rest of the vital functions of the human body. It also "listens" constantly to the surrounding environment. Even when you are deep asleep, your brain is alert for noises, changes in temperature, increases in light intensity, increased vibrations, and a dozen other important signals.

While you are asleep your brain supervises a gigantic factory in which hundreds of enzymes and hormones are manufactured, digestive juices are produced, blood is filtered, and all kinds of chemical solutions are mixed and dissolved. There is also an ultramodern movie studio that operates full blast—producing dreams. If you stop to consider for a moment, a dream is really a sensational achievement. It has color, sound, dialogue, suspense, stunning scene changes, and above all an undeniable emotional impact. Most nights your brain produces the full range of feature films—comedy, drama, suspense, and, occasionally, sensational pornogaphy.

For over a million years human beings slept almost as a natural reflex. In more primitive times a man would wake up at the first light of dawn, work strenuously until sundown, and then fall quickly and deeply asleep at the first darkness. Probably the greatest enemies of natural and uninterrupted sleep were the inventors of artificial light. The candle, the oil lamp, and, later, the electric light bulb destroyed the simple patterns of nature and paved the way for mass insomnia. The normal cycle of brain function—tied to the rising and setting of the sun—was abruptly distorted by the opportunity to stay wide awake until advanced hours of darkness. And the brain resents that kind of distortion.

During the waking hours the brain pulses at a regular rate—both physically and electrically. If you observe a normal living brain you see it expanding and contracting slowly and rhythmically. At the same time it produces a series of electrical impulses known as brain waves, which can be measured and charted as squiggly lines on a graph. Without going into the complicated details of electroence-phalography—which is what the doctors call the squiggles—when a person is about to go to sleep, an entirely different pattern of electrical impulses is produced by the brain. If those patterns do not appear, sleep does not come. That simple—and almost entirely overlooked fact—is the key to overcoming insomnia once and for all.

Insomnia occurs when some event—either inside or outside the brain—interferes with the normal production of sleep-type electrical patterns by the brain. What kinds of events can distort the brain wave patterns? Here are some examples.

*Nervous tension:* Rex, at age thirty-four, is the president of his own high-powered dynamic real estate firm. As he shifts from side to side in his chair, he lifts his expensive tinted glasses to reveal the dark rings under his eyes.

"I know it sounds funny, Doctor, but I just can't stop making deals. It's usually at least ten at night before I can put the phone down, and I don't calm down enough to go to bed until about midnight. And then I spend most of the night lying awake figuring wraparound mortgages, percent returns on investment, depreciation, and time-sharing deals."

Rex shook his head and put his glasses back in place.

"The problem is I usually fall asleep for a couple of hours between three and five in the morning, and when I wake up. I've forgotten all those great angles I worked out during the night!"

Karen has a different but related problem:

"I'm a fashion designer, and you can't believe how cut-throat our business has become lately. It seems that nobody wants to design anymore—they just want to steal! I stay up half the night trying to figure out new and exciting styles, and the other half of the night I can't sleep because I worry that the competition is going to steal my ideas before I can get them to the stores. Unless I get out of this crazy business. I don't think I'm ever going to be able to sleep!

*Fear of insomnia:* Strange as it seems, being afraid that you aren't going to be able to sleep is one of the major factors that may keep you from sleeping. Carl is a typical example:

"You know, about a year ago I went through a crisis in my business and it ruined my sleep pattern. I suffered for almost a month from terrible insomnia. That's when I made up my mind that I'd never allow the same thing to happen again. But I'm almost as bad off now as I was then!"

"Specifically, what's the problem, Carl?"

"Well, everything has to be just right. I mean, the room has to be dark, the neighborhood has to be quiet, and it can't be too hot or too cold. If there's a full moon, I know I'm going to have trouble. If there's a party on the block, I won't sleep a wink until everybody's gone home. If the weather's unusually hot or cold, I'm in for it. If I eat something that upsets me at dinner, I can forget about a good night's sleep from that moment on. I tell you I can't sleep for fear that I'm not going to be able to sleep!"

*Emotional conflicts:* It's amazing how many people pick the hours just before bedtime to bring up controversial topics. Listen to Lydia and see if it sounds at all familiar:

"I just can't believe it! Frank should know better, but almost every night he starts to make trouble just when we're getting ready for bed. Sometimes he complains about my weight. Sometimes he criticizes what I made for dinner. Sometimes he starts in about the kids. I really don't know what to do. I'm damned if I do and I'm damned if I don't!"

"What do you mean, Lydia?"

"Well, if I try to reason with Frank, we end up having a big argument and I don't sleep all night. If I just ignore him, he gets mad and he stays awake tossing and turning all night, and I can't sleep because of all the commotion he's making. What do I do?"

Good question. What does anybody do about insomnia? Well, here's what they do. They take advantage of what we know about the physical and psychological mechanisms of sleep combined with what we know about human nature, and they arrange things so that they sleep—calmly, peacefully and regularly. This is what it involves:

1. *Stop drugging your brain*. The key to conquering insomnia is to adjust the cycle of your brain to the normal cycle of day and night. Beginning immediately after dark, you should try to eliminate all artificial stimuli to your brain. That means you shouldn't smoke, you shouldn't drink, and you shouldn't take any drugs. Since it takes approximately four hours to get those chemicals more or less out of your brain's circulation, be sure to take your last dose of alcohol, tobacco, or drugs (of any kind) at least four hours before you'd like to go to sleep.

2. *Stop overstimulating your brain*. Strange as it may seem, the worst enemy of a good night's sleep can be your television set. Oh yes, I know that some people like to go to sleep watching TV. The dullness and monotony of the programs help to put them in a sleep-trance. But for many people television works just the other way. Why? Well, here's the answer. The image on a TV screen is not like a drawing on a piece of paper. It is actually flickering patterns of light and dark on a screen. That flickering is transmitted directly to your brain, where it strongly influences the rhythm of your brain waves. The TV flicker is so powerful that in some individuals with defects in their brain waves, such as epileptics, it may actually produce powerful seizures or convulsions. You may not have convulsions when you watch some of the stuff on TV, but it may strongly affect the ability of your brain to settle down for the night and sleep.

3. *Establish a regular cycle*. All body functions work best on a regular pattern or rhythm, and sleep is no exception. The best illustration is the way a jet flight through several time zones disturbs the normal biological rhythm and upsets your pattern of sleep. Help your brain to establish a normal sleep cycle by establishing a sleep

pattern according to a regular schedule. Try to go to bed at the same hour every night and follow the same routine.

4. *Avoid exciting nights.* Think about it this way. If your goal is to calm down physically and mentally so that your brain can enjoy its few hours of rest, what good does it do to hop yourself up every night and then hope that your poor brain can somehow overcome the tremendous burden that you place on it? If you're going out for a big night on the town, give yourself an hour or so after you get home before you seriously try to go to sleep. If you have an exciting party at home, take an hour after the last guest leaves to calm down. You'll sleep faster, easier, and longer if you do it that way.

Obviously, the same concept holds true for emotional disturbances. Fight with your spouse, if you have to, in the daylight hours, but leave the night time for sleeping. Think of it this way—if you're rested and relaxed, you'll be able to argue that much better the next day!

5. *Don't be afraid of insomnia.* Losing sleep can't do you any lasting harm—unless you worry about it. Here are the scientific facts:

If you simply lie awake motionless in bed, you get 70 percent as much rest as if you were asleep. So if you lie in bed for ten hours every night *without sleeping a wink* you get the equivalent of seven hours a night sleep. That's more than enough.

If you just relax in bed without worrying about anything, *you will sleep*—much more than you realize. When you *think* that you haven't dozed off for even an instant during a supposedly sleepless night, you have actually slept about half the time. How can I be so sure? Easy. Many dozens of people who complained of insomnia have been observed in sleep laboratories. When they get up in the morning, they insist that they haven't closed their eyes for a moment. But continuous videotapes taken during the night show that they have slept about 50 percent of the time. So don't worry.

6. *Help yourself but let your brain do the rest.* I'll never forget the famous television program on which they promised a contestant $2,000 cash if he could fall asleep within an hour. To make it "easier" for him, they put him on a supersoft mattress with a thousand-dollar bill in each hand. Then they had a twenty-five-piece orchestra playing lullabies at his bedside. Finally, they constructed a wooden bridge above his bed and drove sheep over it one by one so he could count sheep while he fell asleep. Did he fall asleep? What do you think?

The bedroom is for important tasks like sleeping—and sex. Don't let routine chores like business or domestic spats intrude on your sleeping chamber. If you find your mind wandering to business worries when you're ready to sleep, simply send this message to your brain: *"This office is closed until eight o'clock tomorrow morning!"*

You'll be amazed at how well it works!

Oh yes, speaking of sex, that's one of the greatest and most enjoyable weapons against insomnia that you will ever have. The physical and mental tranquillity that a good sexual experience brings makes sleep inevitable and enjoyable. Use that knowledge to make the nights better for you and for your partner as well.

I'd like to continue this chapter but to tell you the truth talking about all these excellent ways to get a good night's sleep has made me just a little bit drowsy. So if you'll excuse me, I think it's time to take a little nap.

# 18
# Loneliness

LONELY. ALONE. LONESOME. LONELINESS. Even the words sound bad—and the experience is much worse. It's like living all by yourself in the middle of the Sahara Desert—with people constantly walking by who don't even know that you exist. It's going home every night to an empty apartment, cooking a tasteless dinner for one, and eating silently before a squawking television set. It's Sunday afternoons by yourself in the park when everyone else is two-by-two. It's showing up at a party alone when everyone else has a partner. It's eating at a restaurant by yourself and reading a book to pretend you don't care. It's all those things and much more—and one *big* thing more. *It's completely unnecessary.*

Whether you like it or not, the facts are these. In the world we live in, being alone comes only as the result of tremendous effort on your part. There are over four billion people on this planet, and at any given moment you have to exclude all of them from your life to qualify as "lonely." To put it another way, if you really suffer from intense prolonged loneliness, you should try your skill at the roulette tables of the world because you are regularly beating odds of over *four billion to one!*

The truth is that being lonely takes time and effort. Let's be honest. People who are constantly lonely have to defend themselves from the threat of finding friends. If you are really dedicated to being lonely, you always have to be on your guard against someone getting friendly with you. Listen to the way Chuck describes it.

In his early thirties, Chuck was dressed in lightly faded jeans, a Lacoste shirt, and a soft woolen polo sweater thrown carelessly across his shoulders. Just barely six feet tall and slender, he slumped down in his chair and spoke slowly in a deep expressive voice:

"You know, it was only when I looked back on it that I realized how much *unconscious* effort I devoted to being lonely. I mean, Doctor, I had it all worked out. First of all, my job. I am—I mean I *was*—a computer programmer. That was great for openers. I spent all day talking to machines, concentrating so hard no one dared to interrupt me, and then going home exhausted every night. What a drag!"

"But you had plenty of free time, didn't you, Chuck?"

"Sure, I did. And I knew how to use that to *stay* lonely. I became a 'computer snob.' Ever hear of that, Doctor?"

"Can't say that I have, Chuck. What's it like?"

Chuck laughed.

"It's like building a brick wall fifty feet high and ten feet thick around yourself—so no one can penetrate your loneliness. You talk nothing but computer slang: 'input,' 'string variables,' 'that won't compute,' and a lot of other junk that no one else understands. The next step is to dress up like your grandfather!"

Chuck pulled a wrinkled snapshot out of his pocket and dropped it on my desk. "See what I mean?"

I saw. It was a man who looked about forty-five years old, dressed in a rumpled tweed jacket. He squinted through gold-rimmed glasses with tiny round lenses. He had long unruly hair, and even in the photo you could see it was long overdue for a shampoo. The pants were baggy and the expression was forlorn.

"That's you?"

"Yep. That's me in my former role of 'professional friend-repellent.' The only living things that dared approach me were moths—and they were only interested in eating my tweed jacket!"

"But how did you pull out of it, Chuck?"

"I didn't, Doctor. That's why I'm here. I'm a smart guy; I know that. But only up to a point. I was tramping around a carnival one Saturday afternoon—alone as usual—and on an impulse I had that picture taken. It shocked the daylights out of me, and I sat down to analyze, computer-fashion, what was wrong with my life. And like everyone with a problem, I got only so far and no farther. I changed the surface, but I know there's a lot more underneath. Now I repel moths more than I do people, but I still can't really make myself part of the world. What's the next step?"

The next step was for Chuck to understand the four basic techniques that people who want to be lonely use to isolate themselves from the rest of the more than four billion human beings that surround them like grains of sand on a beach. Here's the basic blueprint for loneliness:

1. *Lonely people love to be lonely.* They wear isolation like a badge. They say things like "I want to get to know myself," or "Solitude is good for the soul." Sure. There's a time for all that, but it isn't *all* the time. And the worst part for them is that they *repel* potential friends by telling them how *great* it is to be lonely. You've heard this kind of dialogue before, haven't you?

BOY: Hey! What're you doing tonight?

GIRL: Tonight? Well, I was going to read this new book I just bought and listen to a new album.

BOY: Wouldn't you rather get out and move around? You know, see what's going on?

GIRL: (Makes a face) Oh, I don't know. Movies are such

a drag. (Rakes around in her purse for a book of poems. Keeps talking without looking up) Most of those movies are such a waste of time. What's playing?

BOY: (Slowly and silently tiptoes away)

2. *Lonely people are hard to please*. Gloria explains it nicely:

"You know, Doctor, I don't enjoy being lonely, but it's so hard to find someone decent to relate to. After all, I need someone who's intelligent and well educated and attractive and . . ."

"Can I interrupt you for a moment, Gloria?"

Gloria pursed her lips petulantly.

"Well, I suppose so."

"Thank you. Would it be fair to say, Gloria, that you're looking for the Perfect Man?"

"Well, not exactly the *Perfect* Man . . ."

"But something close?"

"Well, maybe . . ."

"But, Gloria. Didn't it ever occur to you that if you do find the Perfect Man, he'll be looking for the Perfect Woman?"

Lonely people are perfectionists like Gloria, and like Gloria, they are constantly looking for perfection in *other* people. Before they resign themselves to a lifelong tour of duty as loyal soldiers in the "vast army of the lonely," they usually pass through a phase where they go through friends like a Great Dane goes through a plate of hamburger. Suddenly—and it happens suddenly—no one can please them. Old friends become worthless and new friends become unworthy. What they are really doing is systematically withdrawing from all human contact in preparation for their blast-off into the trackless wastes of the inner space of solitude—and self-pity. Did I say "self-pity"? Yes, that's an essential ingredient in the psychic recipe book of everyone who's lonely.

3. *Lonely people are martyrs to their loneliness.* It's their one big pleasure in life. Don't believe me? Listen to Helen.

Helen is a slim trim brunette in her very early thirties. She wears a pale beige pants suit; there's a bright silk scarf around her neck knotted through a little gold ring. To say she is attractive is an understatement. Today the only thing *not* attractive about Helen is the expression on her face. The expression is pure annoyance.

"Do you know what it is to be *alone* in Los Angeles, Doctor?"

No, Helen, I don't—and neither do you!"

The annoyance overflowed into her voice.

"Just what do you mean by *that?*

"Just what I said. You can't jump into a swimming pool without getting wet, and you just can't be *alone* in a city of seven million other human beings."

Annoyance intensifing.

"But Doctor! You *know* what I mean!"

"Sure I know what you mean. You mean that you don't have anything to do or anywhere to go or anyone to be with. You feel like you live at the North Pole, with central heating—and a slightly better view."

A thin smile cracked the edges of Helen's lovely lips.

"And taxes that are much too high! Okay, Doctor, I get the idea. I'm all alone in a crowd. It's exactly the feeling I've had since sixth grade—if I have to tell the truth about it. It's as if there's a transparent glass wall between me and all the other people out there. But now that I've confessed, what do we do about it?"

"We identify the basic problems that you and all other lonely people have in common and attack them one by one."

And that's what we're doing.

The final characteristic that all lonely people have in common is this one:

4. *Lonely people are scared.* The amount of fear that

lonely people have varies according to their previous experiences in life, their age, and a host of other things. But there's one thing for sure—as time goes by, fear intensifies and loneliness becomes more and more difficult to deal with. So if you're going to overcome loneliness, there's one ideal time to start. *Now. Right now. This very moment.* Here we go!

Let's get one thing clear right away: *Loneliness is a self-created disease.* It is not the result of heredity, being bitten by a mosquito, or bad luck. *If you are lonely, it is because you did it to yourself and you can undo it if you want to.* The speed with which you overcome your loneliness depends precisely on how badly you want to put it behind you.

Okay, ready to go? What's that? What about society? Doesn't the society you live in make people lonely? It surely does! There are four aspects of so-called modern society that make loneliness a curse:

1. *Competition.* In a culture in which everyone is competing madly against everyone else, loneliness is the order of the day. Envy, greed and mistrust are the vital ingredients of competition; put them together and they spell *l-o-n-e-l-y.*

2. *Industrialization.* Efficient industry requires massive dehumanization. Instead of people, you deal with computers, machines, recorded announcements and TV monitors. Day by day people become more and more isolated from each other.

3. *Social models.* A "social model" is simply the example that is held up for everyone to follow. Our models are given to us on television, in the movies, in school and where we work—among other places. The most common social model these days—the example we are encouraged to follow—*is the loner.* That's the person who doesn't need anyone or anything. He or she is typically tall, aloof and aggressive. These models are indifferent to most hu-

man contacts and relate only to other people like them. In reality, most of these people are so sick that they cannot survive outside of cigarette or cosmetic ads. Fortunately, there are very few real people like that.

4. *The class structure*. Even in the most supposedly democratic societies, there is a rigid class structure in operation. Often it depends on family background or ethnic origin. In more materialistic societies, the class barriers depend on money and social position. (In case you wondered, social position is determined by who gives the fanciest parties.) Even in a democratic nation like the United States, these inflexible class distinctions prevent the dozens of casual daily contacts that everyone has from blossoming into friendships.

So, that means loneliness isn't all a person's fault. Right? *Wrong!* It means only that the crazy society you live in makes it easy for you to fulfill your wish to be lonely. And even more important, now that you know what some of the built-in obstacles are, it's going to be easier for you to overcome them. Ready? Let's go!

The very first step is to *turn off your people-repellent!* Stop generating those invisible vibrations that scream *"Get away from me!"* to anyone who dares approach within two feet of you. You don't think you do that? Okay, try this little experiment.

Take a snapshot of yourself—nothing fancy, an instant camera will do fine. But don't smile. Be very careful to get your standard expression—straight on, the way you look to people who meet you for the first time. Put the picture aside. Then take another photo. But this time, look *friendly. Warm, open, outgoing!* Let all of your real personality come right out in your expression. Now compare the two photos. If they're the same, you're in big trouble! (Just kidding. If you've been honest they won't be.)

Now you see, undeniably, a big part of the problem. Anyone who sees your face gets the message that you're not eager for human contact—to put it mildly. All right, let's carry this little experiment one step further. Tomorrow—or the very next time you launch yourself into that big world out there—put on your *friendly* face to everyone you meet. Almost. That doesn't include, of course, a panhandler who accosts you on the corner or every weirdo who sidles up to you. But it does include every other relatively rational human being.

Be nice to cabdrivers, ticket collectors, bank tellers, store clerks, folks who ask directions, everyone you work with, the people you meet casually at coffee breaks and business meetings. That also applies to telephone conversations. At least part of the time, it's another *person* who's talking to you—not some zombie recording. (If you're *sure* it's a recording, you can be mean. But be *sure*. Unfortunately, these days, more and more people sound like recordings—but that's why we're discussing all this.)

Now don't expect miracles; that's another problem of loneliness. It seems that many lonely people suffer from the Prince/Princess Charming syndrome. They are always expecting the sound of pounding hooves right outside their bedroom door as their one and only rides up on a white horse. To be honest, the odds are against that. What I can *guarantee* is that the first day you get rid of that acrid aroma of the people-repellent you've been wearing, your life will change. You'll find yourself surrounded by friends—at least in the superficial sense—and not by strangers. Ninety-nine percent of the folks out there are just as eager for real human contact as you are; you'll see what I mean as soon as you try it.

The next step is to form some more lasting relationships—as they used to say in college. A good place to start is by listing the places *not* to go. Here are some of them:

1. *Singles clubs*
2. *Church organizations*
3. *Group therapy organizations*

4. *Clubs for divorced, separated, or widowed people*
5. *Singles apartments*
6. *Any other groupings of people designed to bring lonelies together.*

Surprised? No, not with what you *know* about loneliness now. These are *precisely* the groups that attract lonely people—with all their problems and their inner desire to stay lonely. I know what you're thinking of: All those wonderful movies in which a lonely guy and a lonely gal meet in the public library and all of a sudden they're not lonely anymore. They've found each other! Sorry, that's only a movie. In real life when you get twenty-five lonely people together at a party or a picnic, they spray so much "Keep away!" juice on each other that you can hardly breathe. If anybody ever invites you to one of those "singles groups," run as fast and as far as you can in the other direction. At least you might bump into a normal person while you're running.

The groups that you *want* are the ones that attract dynamic outgoing men and women, who never think about being isolated or alone. Here are some of the good choices—and if they don't turn you on enough, keep reading. I'll give you a supersensational never-fail choice before we finish this chapter. If you try it and you're still lonely—well, all I can say is, you won't be!

Here are the easy choices first:

1. *Any political organization—your choice.* These are generally groups that play for keeps, and there is no room for wasting time. But be sure and pick the main organization—don't fall in with "Women for Watkins" or "Executives for Better Government." Get right into the Democratic or Republican or Vegetarian party organization and work your head off. You'll be amazed that your loneliness will disappear within a week or so at the most—and guess

what? You'll be helping the cause of democracy at the same time!

2. *Active social-welfare organizations.* That doesn't mean the passive "better government" groups made up mostly of married women who want reasonably to fill up their spare time. It means active militant social-progress groups—and it's up to you to choose the political orientation. Antinuclear, proabortion, pronuclear, anti-abortion—it's all a personal matter. But you will be with serious people in a serious cause—and there's no room for loneliness. Pick your group carefully. Make sure that it agrees with your personal convictions and that it won't get you into trouble. Then tear right in! Goodbye to loneliness forever!

3. A *new job.* Stop for a moment and analyze what you do for a living. Maybe—before you really thought about it carefully—you fell into a line of work that keeps you away from the rest of the human race. The typing pool? Routine office work? Working in a factory? A warehouse? Same fifteen faces every day. Same work, same future. Nope. The world is full of opportunities to meet the rest of its inhabitants. Here are some of the possibilities that kill loneliness on the spot.

Think of working as an airline ticket agent, restaurant hostess, or salesman, or in a travel agency, in public relations, hotel work, retail sales, and similar public contact occupations. Okay, I know. You don't have any experience; you'll earn less money; those kinds of jobs are below you, et cetera, et cetera, et cetera. Well, let's just keep one little thing in mind. This isn't a career conference. This is a war against the agony of being alone. If you find a job that fills your days with friendship, camaraderie, and dozens of shared experiences, who cares about ten dollars a week more or less?

Let me give you a few examples of my former patients who switched occupations and what it did for them:

1. Interior decorator to waitress at an exclusive restaurant: 25 percent increase in salary, and depression replaced by enthusiasm.

2. Author of textbooks to junior college professor: same salary and a life filled with warm human contacts.

3. Private secretary to airline ticket agent: a whole new world of free travel and excitement. Ten percent increase in salary.

4. Data processing supervisor to civilian police department data processing planner: the feeling of being wanted—of being a part of a team for the first time in his life. Ten percent cut in salary compensated by pension and medical plan.

Okay, maybe a job change isn't fast enough for you. Maybe after reading this far you've decided you don't want to be lonely a moment longer than necessary. Well, I have to take my hat off to you, and here is a superinstant solution to loneliness as promised—tried and tested many times over by my patients. It takes a little more courage than average, but it gives supersensational results. If you can pull it off, your problems will be over in two shakes of a lamb's tail. Here we go:

*Go back to school—but with a difference.* By careful planning, arrange a set of circumstances that will make everything go exactly the way you want it to. For example, do what Lois did:

"All right, you were right and I was wrong, Doctor!"

"What do you mean by that, Lois?"

Lois smiled and fluffed her short blonde hair.

"I think you know, you sly old doctor! You sent me to welding school!"

"Well, it wasn't exactly welding school, Lois. It was just a welding course in an adult education class at the local junior college. Wasn't that it?"

Lois chuckled.

"It was the atomic bomb, that's what it was! I know

how I came here. Wilted, miserable, really feeling all alone in the world. You put me in a class with sixteen men—four engineers, two doctors, a dentist, six fellows that were starting their own businesses, a wonderful man who manufactures sailboats, and two sculptors. Only one was married—and that was one of the sculptors. After twelve weeks I had eighteen new friends, more social life than I could manage, and . . ."

"Just a minute, Lois. You said there were sixteen men and you ended up with eighteen new friends. How could that be?"

"Oh, Doctor, you weren't listening! Remember one of the sculptors was married and he has such a nice wife! We see each other at least once a week."

"And the eighteenth friend?"

"Well, every class has to have an instructor, doesn't it? And one more benefit that I never even expected!"

"What was that, Lois?"

"I guess it almost got lost in the shuffle. I learned to weld!"

Lois won every step of the way. She set up the situation so that everything was in her favor. She was young, bright and blonde—the only woman in a group of above-average men. That's the kind of thing that almost every lonely person can do to shift the odds suddenly in their favor. For men, it works the same way.

Walt was medium height with dark brown hair that always seemed to fall over his forehead. His brown eyes sparkled excitedly as he spoke:

"You know, I thought you were crazy, Doctor. I'm a professor of chemistry, and you sent me to beauticians' school! If I hadn't been so miserable and so desperate, I would've run out of here and looked for a sane doctor!"

"If you hadn't been so miserable and so desperate, I wouldn't have sent you to beauticians' school! For drastic disease, drastic medicine! How'd it work out?"

Walt shrugged.

"Much better than I expected. First, there were twenty-five of the most beautiful girls I had ever seen. There must be something about beauty school that attracts beauties! Then, the unexpected happened."

"What was that?"

"They started *fighting* over me! After the second week we had to practice on men's hair, and I was the only man there—except for some old retired guys who came in from time to time for a haircut. Imagine me, Walter, the lonely little college professor, with twenty-five really great girls pushing and shoving to work on him. Of course, I accommodated them all."

"How did you do that?"

"Haven't you ever heard of homework, Doctor? I took pity on the ones that were most desperate and allowed them to come over to my house after school to practice on me. They were all pretty nice about it. They brought me cookies and doughnuts, and some of the girls made dinner for me one night. I helped them and they helped me."

Walter broke out in a smile that stretched from one end of his face to the other—and kept growing. Then he became serious.

"As you can imagine, I'm not going to be a beautician. But I'm not going back to being a chemistry professor either."

"What are you going to do?"

"I'm going to combine the two, Doctor. The beauty business these days is more chemistry than anything else, and those girls are so sweet. I mean, aside from the obvious, I really enjoy being around happy young girls instead of grouchy old professors and bored chemistry students. So, I'm opening my own beauty school. The best of both worlds—thanks to a crazy suggestion from a not-so-crazy doctor."

Well, that's it. You didn't get lonely in one day, and you mustn't expect to overcome your loneliness in a mere twenty-four hours. But you're on your way. You understand more about the problem than ever before, and you have two very powerful weapons at your disposal. They are the experiences of others who have overcome the same problem that troubles you and a myriad of effective techniques to use to help yourself!

# 19
# Money

"MONEY—THAT'S THE WORD! And what a strange word it is! *M-o-n-e-y*. To most of us it means dollars or francs or rubles or pesos—coins and bills all jingling together. It means checking accounts and bars of gold and gilt-edged securities. How wrong we are! *Money* is all of that and none of that. *Money* is something far more basic: *Money* is simply the difference between life and death, between happiness and misery, between sickness and health. *Money* is the basis of every human evil and every human good. All wars are fought for *money*, and the greatest lies in the history of the world have been told for *money*. If you are ever going to make money, have money, save money, or manage money, you must first understand what money *is*. And *this* is what it is: Money is *concentrated power*—no more and no less.

Look at it this way. How much weight can you lift? A hundred pounds? Two hundred pounds? Maybe. I can lift five hundred pounds with two fingers. How do I do it? Easy. I just take four ten-dollar bills out of my wallet, and four big strong men come and lift the five hundred pounds for me. I have concentrated the force of four human beings into four pieces of paper.

Can you fly through the air like a bird? I can. I don't even have to flap my wings. I make a telephone call and mention a little number engraved on a plastic wafer. In an hour I am on an airplane on my way to Manila, Helsinki, or Bogotá. It is the power of money that makes me fly. I have concentrated the power of fifty thousand horses into a small credit card which is nothing else than *plastic* money.

Even the number of your days on earth depends on the amount of money you have. If you have enough money, you can buy the best food, the best medical care, the best climate, the best housing—the best of everything to make your life long and happy. If you don't have enough money, you breathe polluted air, you eat bad food, you wait long hours at charity medical clinics, you suffer icy winters in drafty tenements.

So all you need to be really happy is a lot of money? Not quite. You need intelligence, maturity, understanding, and experience to find lasting happiness. But if you don't have money, all those things won't get you a cup of coffee. So just get the money—and the rest of the qualities— and you're all set? That's right—except for one little catch. There is a limited amount of money in the world and a lot of people who want it. To make matters worse, the ones who have a lot of money are engaged in a constant battle to keep *you* from getting any. And they don't stop there. They are even trying to get what little money you may have away from you. How? Listen to Bill.

The gray flannel slacks and the blue wool blazer were striking. The silk tie with its maroon and gold diagonal stripes completed the uniform. The shoes were finely sewn cordovan loafers; the socks were pale gray silk with little clocks.

Bill flipped open his engine-turned eighteen-karat-gold cigarette case and tipped it toward me. The cigarettes were Turkish.

"No thanks, Bill."

He shrugged and flicked his enamel and gold DuPont lighter. The flame surged upward, and the room filled with the acrid aroma of Latakia tobacco.

"Would you mind if I guessed what you are going to say, Bill?"

Bill grinned good-naturedly.

"What is this, psychiatry or mental telepathy? Sure, go ahead."

"You're going to tell me that no matter how much money you make you don't seem to be able to save a penny."

Bill drew hard on his cigarette and then suddenly gound it out in the ashtray on my desk.

"Save? I only wish that were it! I go deeper in debt every five minutes! Look, I make one hundred twenty-five thousand dollars a year. I don't have a nickel in savings, and I've even borrowed out all my insurance policies."

Bill held his wallet high in the air and let the accordion-pleated plastic compartments fall free. There were at least a dozen credit cards flapping in the breeze.

"I can buy anything I want, but I can't seem to save a penny. There—I said it! Look, I'm fifty-eight years old and I can't keep working forever. I'm a salesman—I sell corporate aircraft, you know, company airplanes—and there's no pension plan for me. I'm supposed to live on Social Security? Sitting in the park all day with the rest of the seniles while the pigeons go doo-doo on my old gray head? Listen. I'm used to living well. I couldn't take that kind of life!"

"Bill, exactly what do you mean by 'living well'?"

Bill was shocked.

"Well you know living *well!* A trip to France every summer, skiing every winter, a nice house, and a place in the country. A car for the city and a sports car—maybe two. Eating out a couple of times a week. Good private schools for the kids. Entertaining my friends. After all I work hard and I deserve it!"

"I'm sure you do. Tell me something else, Bill. What's the number one *purpose* of money?"

Raised eyebrows.

"Why, to buy things, of course!"

"Okay, Bill, that's your problem. Buying things is purpose number *four* of money. The number *one* purpose of money is to keep you alive. Its goal is to buy you the minimum level of food, shelter, and safety. It functions to give you a roof over your head, to give you enough food to keep your mind and body operating, and to give you access to lawyers, doctors, and employers. The number *two* purpose of money is to educate you—in the broadest sense of the word 'educate.' It gives you the means to obtain the information and facts and skills that allow you to operate successfully in this world. That can range all the way from buying a newspaper to getting a college degree."

Bill's eyes were a little glassy.

"Are you still with me?"

He nodded.

"I guess so. This is pretty heavy stuff for a guy like me, who never hung on to a ten-dollar bill for more than an hour or so. But keep going, it's fascinating!"

"Fine. Here we go. The third purpose of money is to *make more money!* As you probably may have noticed, money doesn't fall from the sky. If all you do is work for a salary, you are using up a totally nonrenewable resource—*yourself!* With every salary check you collect, you have one less week of your life to sell."

Bill interrupted.

"What do you mean, 'one less week of your life to sell'? I'm not selling weeks."

"No? Just think about it a minute. When you have a job, no matter what it is, you only have so many hours or weeks or months that you can *sell* until you can't work anymore. Your boss buys your services at a fixed rate— ten dollars an hour, five hundred dollars a week, one hundred and twenty-five thousand dollars a year. Even if you work on commission, you get paid in proportion to the time you put in. Although you may not like to think about it, Bill, during your lifetime you have only so many hours or weeks or months to work—or to sell. So you *are* selling weeks. And when you can't sell them any more, you can't collect any more money.''

Bill looked depressed.

''But cheer up! That's the point of the third purpose of money. Sooner or later your ability to 'sell weeks' is going to conk out. *But the ability of your money to make more money lives forever*. Take a simple example. If you put a thousand dollars in a bank account at ten percent interest, those one thousand big dollars give birth to one hundred little dollars every year. Even more interesting, those little dollars are born whether you go to work or not. To make the prospect even more exciting, even after you are gone, those big dollars are still making little dollars. It doesn't stop there. If you leave them alone, at the end of the first year you can add the hundred dollars in interest to the thousand dollars on deposit and the little dollars become big ones because they too can *reproduce*. The second year they give birth to one hundred and *ten* dollars, the third year one hundred and *twenty-one* dollars, and so on. How much interest does your gold cigarette case pay? What's the percent return on those gourmet dinners in those fancy restaurants?

Bill seemed annoyed.

''But, Doctor, 'Man does not live by bread alone.' You have to feed the soul as well as the body.''

''I'm delighted that you mentioned that, Bill. That's what I meant when I said that the people who have most of the money are working night and day to get yours away from you. How do you expect to 'feed your soul' a few years from now when you're sitting in the park ducking doo-doo from the pigeons? Remember, Bill, those were your words, not mine. I don't think that four hundred dollar sport jacket of yours will stand too much pigeon poop."

Bill smiled.

"I think I understand, Doctor."

"I hope so, Bill. One of the most dramatic achievements of modern communications has been to convince people to buy things they don't really *need*. The most common technique is to hide the real purpose of a material object."

Bill interrupted eagerly.

"Like a cigarette case, for example?"

"Right! If you're going to smoke, that little pasteboard box the cigarettes come in keeps them out of the rain for the time it takes to smoke them. The gold cigarette case doesn't improve the flavor—or protect you from cancer, if you don't mind a medical point of view."

Bill was hanging in there—he was still smiling.

"But what if I really *want* a gold cigarette case, Doctor?"

"That's okay with me. But you'll do yourself a favor if you ask yourself *why* you want it. And then if you still want it, *pay for it out of money that you don't have to earn.*"

"You mean those big dollars that give birth to little dollars?"

"Right. If you sell your weeks to pay for necessities and use the proceeds of your investments to pay for all those little toys that you just can't resist, you won't have to spend your golden years shivering on a park bench waiting for the cut-rate cafeteria to open."

"What do you consider 'little toys,' Doctor?"

"What do *you* think, Bill?"

"While you were talking I was trying to analyze it. One example I thought of was my sports car. Like you said, when they want to sell you something you don't need, they hide the real purpose. The purpose of a car is to transport you from one place to another. I guess about the worst way to accomplish that is to use a three hundred horsepower engine in a fifty thousand dollar chassis. But they sell you the romance; as the owner of a Ferrari, I can testify to that!''

"You're on the right track. All those wonderful little gadgets that you don't really need are 'little toys.' You can include your DuPont lighter that must have set you back two hundred and fifty dollars . . .''

"Three-twenty, Doc.''

"Okay, three-twenty. Your country house is more like a 'big toy.' Figure how much you use it, and maybe you'd be better off renting someone else's country house. But that's not your biggest problem now.''

Bill looked puzzled.

"What's my biggest problem?''

"Getting yourself on an even keel financially. Like you said, you have only so many more weeks to sell before you head for the park. Try this plan and see how it works for you.''

1. *Live beneath your income.* Instead of spending like a man who earns $125,000 a year, try spending like someone who makes $50,000. You'll be amazed to find that your standard of living won't go down nearly as fast as your bank balance will go up.

2. *Don't waste energy.* Remember that every dollar you spend comes from your own sweat. When you buy that giant-screen television with remote control and built-in video-cassette recorder, it costs you much more than money. It costs you at least a month of your life—calling on customers, arguing, convincing, struggling. The money that you earn is nothing more than the physical and mental energy that you have expended—concentrated into paper certificates. If you waste money, you waste your own very limited supply of energy.

3. *Plastic does not bring happiness.* Don't fool yourself into believing that *any* material object will bring happiness. I know the message in those full-page ads and the TV commercials: "I was miserable until I got my microwave

oven or my five-way hair curler or my octaphonic stereo or my instant color camera or . . ." I'm sure you can add plenty more items to that list. Don't be fooled by the smiles on the faces of the people in the ads. They're not grinning wildly because the product gives them a permanent high. They're grinning because it's hard to get a job as a model and they're happy to be working. Your happiness in this life depends on what you accomplish, your relationships with the people you love, and what you contribute to the world around you. There is *nothing* you can buy that will assure you personal fulfillment.

4. *Don't buy anything unless you need it.* Remember the story about the man who wanted to get better gas mileage in his car? He bought a special filter that added three miles per gallon. Then he bought a new distributor that added five miles a gallon. He installed a new carburetor to add seven miles per gallon. A fancy muffler was guaranteed to give him another four miles per gallon. You know what finally happened? His gas tank *overflowed*.

Before you buy *anything* make sure you need it. If you invest in a special microwave oven to save electricity, it may take you a mere ten years to pay back your investment from the electricity you save. Selling your wasteful big old car and buying a nice economical new little car may eat up your savings on gasoline for the next nine years. *Saving* money can be a comfortable alibi for *spending* money. Make sure you're not kidding yourself. Don't buy something because it's a bargain. Don't buy it because you think it might save you money. Buy it because you need it and you can't do without it. If you do it that way, you'll have more to enjoy and you'll enjoy it more.

5. *Remember your priorities.* First, take care of your needs for good wholesome food. Second, get yourself a safe comfortable place to live. Third, put enough cash aside to provide for emergencies. (Incidentally, in spite of what those ads say, a credit card *isn't* emergency cash.

Credit cards have this nasty habit of being cut off just when you need them the most.) The next level of priorities is to get yourself the education and knowledge you need. In this modern world your education must be continuous. You have to learn about your business or profession. You have to learn about money. You have to learn about economic trends. You have to learn about how to cope in a world that seems to get crazier every day. The third category of priority is to use your money to make more money. That's tied right in with priority number two. But remember, most of the gambling these days is *not* done in the casinos. It's done in the stock market, in the commodities market, in real estate, in mutual funds, in tax shelters. For every person who has ten thousand dollars there are at least ten thousand sharpies trying to get it away from him. Study investments and investing and learn what's safe and what's not safe. There's no point to saving and sacrificing if you end up making a bad investment and losing it all. (Safe investments change from month to month. Government bonds may be excellent today and a month from now they may be unrewarding. Inflation tends to change all the rules overnight. If you would like a *current* list of recommended investments, you are welcome to write to me in care of Scott Meredith, 845 Third Avenue, New York, New York 10022.)

As we said in the beginning, money is *power*. If you don't have it, you are powerless. If you do have it, you are *powerful*. You can do it either way—which do you prefer?

# 20
# Obesity

OBESITY IS NOT a description—it's a diagnosis. Being fat is not an accident—it's a lifestyle. Being overweight means a lot more than just dressing in dark colors and sweating a lot. When you get fat you set in motion a long chain of circumstances that makes your life completely different from the lives of people of normal weight.

When you get fat—say 25 percent over your ideal body weight—you bring on some big changes in the way your body functions. These are some of them:

1. *Your appetite for food begins to change.* Thin people feel satisfied after a relatively small meal, but fat people can eat and eat without reaching the natural level of satisfaction that stops their desire for more food. I learned that the hard way about twenty-five years ago with a patient named Grace.

With her beautiful blonde hair and baby blue eyes, at twenty-nine Grace looked just like a doll—a slightly over-stuffed doll, to be sure. She was easily 220 pounds and gaining fast.

"Grace, think of it this way. When you start to eat something, the first bite is always the best. The second

159

bite isn't quite as good, and by the time you've eaten ten bites of something, you're hardly tasting it. Now let's try a little experiment. What's your favorite food?''

Her always cheerful face broke into a wide grin.

"Banana cream pie!"

"Fine. Let's try it this way. Tomorrow buy yourself a big banana cream pie. At lunch time sit down with the pie and a pencil and paper. Slice yourself a piece of pie and eat it and write down how it tastes. Then slice another piece of pie and eat that and write down the way it tastes to you. Do that as many times as you think makes sense. Okay?''

The grin got wider.

"Sure, Doctor! It's a great idea!''

A week later Grace was back, a little fatter and clutching a piece of paper in her plump little hand.

"How did it go?''

"Fine! Can we do it again this week?''

"Well, first let's see how it turned out. Would you like to read the list?''

"Sure! Here it is! 'First piece—tastes wonderful! Second piece—great! Third piece—delicious! Fourth piece—super! Fifth piece—luscious! . . .''

"Just a minute, Grace. How many pieces of pie did you eat?''

Innocent smile.

"Why, twelve pieces, Doctor. You only told me to buy one pie!''

"Ah, yes, Grace. And how did the twelfth piece taste?''

Grace pretended to frown as she consulted her list.

"Hmmm, let me see. Oh yes, here it is 'Twelfth piece— sensational! I could eat a dozen more!' ''

2. *Your appetite for sex begins to change.* As more and more of the tissues and organs of your body are converted to fat your endocrine glands begin to slow down. Men gradually lose their sexual potency, and women have less and less interest in sex. There is also a strange and gradual

shift in secondary sexual characteristics toward the opposite sex. Fat men have less body hair and smoother skin than thinner men, and fat women begin to show more facial and body hair than women of normal weight. This is probably a result of suppression of the ovaries and testicles as a result of the metabolic distortions caused by the excessive adipose tissue. That often starts a vicious cycle since the loss of sexual gratification pushes many fat people to eat more in an attempt to get their satisfaction wherever they can.

3. *Obesity produces mental changes.* You know the old saying "Fat people are always friendly because they can't run fast!" Well, that's only an ironic way of describing the well-known personality changes that almost all fat people undergo. Generally, fat people are *superficially* cheerful and outgoing. Why? Well, first of all, they have to be. Since they are not as physically attractive as people of normal weight, they must project more personal charm just to get by. For someone who is fat, getting and *keeping* a job, making and *keeping* friends, and getting along with their family are more complicated and demanding than they are for thin people. Secondly, although it may not look that way on the surface, most fat people are depressed. If you have close friends who are fat, you know what I mean. They may put on a good show for the outside world, but down deep they don't have much to be euphoric about.

Charlie expresses it well: "Ho-ho-ho!"

Charlie's double chins jiggled as he laughed.

"I really don't know why I'm here, Doctor! Never felt better in my life! Say, did you hear the one about the man whose wife was so fat that when she sat around the house she really sat around the house?"

More laughing and more jiggling of chins.

"What kind of work do you do, Charlie?"

"Insurance is my game, Doctor. Life insurance. I've

sold a million dollars a year in policies every year for the past ten years! Now I know what you're going to say—'You have to die to win.' "

Charlie chuckled good-naturedly.

"Nothing could be farther from the truth. Life insurance is the best investment in the world, let me tell you. Let's make a deal? You make me thin and I'll make you rich!"

"We'll talk about that later. But right now, what brought you to my office?"

"A great big taxicab with heavy-duty springs!"

More guffaws. It was time to take another tack.

"Charlie, how much do you really weigh?"

Charlie put on a mock-serious expression.

"On a real hot day about twenty-one pounds, I'd say."

"Twenty-one pounds?"

Hard chuckles.

"Sure, Doc. Once you melt all the fat off, there's not much left!"

We weren't really making progress.

"How long have you been so depressed, Charlie?"

Absolute silence. No smiles. No laughs. Double chins frozen in place. Finally a weak little voice squeaked: "About ten years, I guess. I didn't know it showed."

"Cheer up, Charlie, maybe it's only obvious to me. Look, depression is the single most common symptom in fat people. Being fat like you are . . . By the way, how much do you really weigh?"

Tiny voice: "Two hundred seventy-seven."

"How tall are you?"

"Five feet six inches."

"How old are you now?"

Very weak voice: "Fifty-three next birthday."

"Now it begins to make sense, doesn't it? You're fifty-three years old and a hundred pounds overweight. You have high blood pressure, right?"

"Yes. How did you know?"

"If you're a hundred pounds overweight, you almost

*have* to have high blood pressure. You have a touch of diabetes . . .''

Charlie winced.

"Sugar in the urine every once in a while?"

He nodded.

"Your sex life leaves something to be desired."

Charlie almost smiled for the first time in ten minutes.

"That's the understatement of the year! It leaves a *lot* to be desired!"

"And to add insult to injury you're selling *life insurance!* Did you ever read that bulletin put out by the medical department of your own company that says that after the age of forty-five, for every ten pounds of extra weight, you increase your chances of dying by one percent?"

Charie frowned.

"Well, that's a lot of bunk! That's just doctors' double-talk! It doesn't mean anything!"

"Wait a minute, Charlie! What happened to the jolly fat man?"

The frown deepened.

"Okay, Charlie, take it easy. You and I both know that your smiles and jokes are part of the fat man's defense mechanism. It's about time to face your problem. Let's leave it at this: Ask yourself if your company would insure a man like you."

Charlie didn't say a word. He just pressed his lips together and slowly shook his head from side to side.

Six months later he was in my office again—on his last visit. He was ninety-seven pounds lighter and really in a good mood.

"Okay, you won, Doc!"

"No, you won, Charlie."

Big smile.

"You're right. No more diabetes, no more high blood pressure, no more depression—and I just sold myself a life insurance policy last week. But there's one last bone I want to pick with you. For all the times I've been coming to you, you always called me *f-a-t!* Why don't you ever use a more polite word, like 'obese,' for instance?''

It was my turn to smile.

"I'll tell you the truth, Charlie. It's because I like to talk English to my patients. That gentle little word 'obese' comes from the Latin word *obesus*. And in Latin *obesus* means nothing else than *f-a-t!*''

Charlie laughed, and that gave him the last laugh—in more ways than one!

All right. Suppose you're fat and you want to get thin. The first step is to have a physical exam to eliminate the one-in-a-million chance that you might have some physical reason for being fat. It's a good idea to establish once and for all that you don't have a thyroid problem or some other excuse. Then the next step is to go on a diet. To everyone at that point the *big* question seems to be, Which diet? Actually, that's the *little* question. The *little* question? How can it be? There are so many diets to choose from! There's the egg diet and the grapefruit diet, the high carbohydrate diet, the low carbohydrate diet, the water diet, the alcohol diet, the Mayo Clinic diet, the Naval Academy diet, the police diet, the pumpkin diet, and on and on and on.

Well, if you're going to lose weight and *keep it off*, there's only *one* diet. I call it the *diet-diet*.

1. *To lose weight you must eat less*. The seductive appeal of most of those exotic weight-reduction diets is the hope that you can ''eat all you want'' and still lose weight. That's true if all you want to eat is foam rubber or candy wrappers. But if you want to eat food and you eat all you want, you will get fat. You made yourself fat by eating too much, and the only way you can make yourself thin is by eating too little—for a while.

2. *To lose weight you must eat well*. Your weight-reduction diet must consist of high-quality food that nourishes your mind and body on a lower caloric intake. If

your diet is half junk, then your body has to get 100 percent of its nourishment from 50 percent of what you are eating. Most fad diets fail in the long run because they don't nourish your mind (which is an organ, the brain) *and* your body. If your brain is deprived of its nutrition, it can't control the rest of you and keep you on your diet. Eating high-quality food doesn't mean munching on fancy brand names or high-fashion items like kiwi fruit or tofu. It means simply fresh fruits and vegetables (remember those?), whole grains, and no junk foods.

3. *To lose weight permanently you must go on a lifetime diet.* If you live on boiled coconuts and raw spinach for a month, you'll take off weight. But as soon as you go back on a diet of white bread, refined sugar, cola drinks, and all the rest, that weight will come creeping back on. And each time, it gets harder and harder to take off. (You've noticed that, haven't you?) If you want to bring your weight down to normal and keep it there, you have to pick a good sound diet and make it your way of life. The one I like the best is a little diet I put together called *The Save Your Life Diet* (Random House, 1975). It's a simple diet program that consists of just the fresh fruits and vegetables, the whole grains, and the other items we mentioned in the section above. It is, of course, a high-fiber diet, which is important for many reasons—including the protection it gives from cancer and heart attacks and the built-in safeguards that will effectively prevent you from ever getting fat again. It's an easy diet to stay on—more than half the people in the world follow it all their lives and they are healthier than we are.

4. *To lose weight, you must make the choice.* You have to take the deliberate decision to make your life better. That would seem to be an easy decision. On the one hand, you have to give up greasy hamburgers, sickly sweet candy bars, gooey white bread, and, of course, banana cream pie. On the other hand, you give up the need to shop in stores for fat people, trips to the doctor to have

your diabetes checked, the prospect of significantly short-ening your life, and all the other trials and tribulations of being fat. What it really boils down to is this: If you don't *want* to be fat, you don't *have* to be fat. The decision is yours. Slimness—and everything that goes with it—is only a mouthful away.

# 21
# Premature Ejaculation

THE ONLY PEOPLE in this world who *suffer* from premature ejaculation are women. They're the ones who miss all the fun. In contrast a man who ejaculates too fast gets it all—erection, stimulation, orgasm, and ejaculation. It's the woman who is left high—and not-so-dry.

As one of my premature-ejaculating patients once observed:

"Doctor, premature ejaculation isn't all that bad—if only my wife wouldn't complain so much!"

But that, of course, *is* the problem. Wives and girl friends do complain—and with very good reason. Sylvia expresses it eloquently.

Sylvia was what they call "California Gold." Her golden tan skin contrasted with her short blonde hair and her bright blue eyes. She was about twenty-seven years old, and she more than filled out her too-tight designer jeans and her one-size-too-small white cotton T-shirt. As she leaned over my desk, she spoke with real emotion:

"Dr. Reuben, you can't imagine how terrible it is! I really like sex—I won't deny that. But I don't get any!"

She bit her pretty little lower lip.

"I mean, I get it but it doesn't do me any good. Jim,

my husband, is great in bed but not great enough for me. Sometimes I get within seconds of climaxing—and then he comes and it's all over! You can imagine where that leaves me! Then I have to do the best I can for myself and—well, to be honest, that's not why I got married.''

Sylvia is right of course. And what does Jim have to say? Listen:

"Gee, Doctor, I don't know. I guess I love Sylvia and I don't want to do her any harm, but it must be something wrong with my penis. I just can't seem to hold back, and no matter how fast she can reach her orgasm, I have mine just a little faster. Yep, it must have something to do with my penis. . . .''

Premature ejaculation has *nothing* to do with the penis, *nothing* to do with the prostate gland, *nothing* to do with the secretion of male hormones or any other part of the body below the eyebrows. Premature ejaculation is a direct result of a specific message sent from the brain to the part of the spinal cord that controls the timing of ejaculation. That message says: *"Three, two, one—blast off! Right now!"*

And it blasts off, *right now!*

Now let's get down to cases. How do you define premature ejaculation? Like every other aspect of human emotional functioning, a useful definition depends on who, what, and where. If a man ejaculates in four minutes but his wife reaches her orgasm in three minutes fifty-five seconds, as far as she is concerned his ejaculation is right on schedule. But if he ejaculates thirty seconds or five thrusts after starting intercourse, he has premature ejaculation.

There are limits in the other direction as well. If a woman takes an hour to climax and her husband just can't hold out that long, he doesn't really have premature ejaculation. To complicate things just a tiny bit, some men have premature ejaculation with their wives and not with their girl friends or vice versa. Some men ejaculate superfast with prostitutes while others can last only with a prostitute. That in itself proves—if there ever were any doubt—that premature ejaculation is an emotional and not a physical problem. Generally speaking, if a man takes less than five to ten minutes to ejaculate, with less than fifty to one hundred pelvic thrusts, he probably has premature ejaculation.

Okay, now what do we do about it? Well, if you ejaculate prematurely, obviously the first step in getting over it is to understand what it really is.

1. *Premature ejaculation is getting even with women.* No matter how much you may love a woman consciously, if you give her the P.E. treatment, you're getting back at her for something. She may always get her own way, she may win all the arguments, she may have equal rights, but when it comes to the most vital of male-female relationships, you're giving her the works. Or better said, you're *not* giving her the works. The basic goal of P.E. is to deny a woman *the greatest of all physical satisfactions*—orgasm.

2. *The penis has nothing to do with premature ejaculation.* That's why any solution based on physical principles has to fail. Smearing a local anesthetic ointment on the tip of your penis is silly; if you could smear it on the tip of your brain you might get better results. The much-publicized sex clinic "squeeze technique" is laughable. Remember the articles about how the woman should masturbate the man and then, at the moment just before orgasm, she's supposed to pinch the head of his penis *hard! Ouch!* All that does is substitute a sadomasochistic maneuver for an emotional malfunction. Nope, the problem isn't located in the head of your penis—it's located in the head that's on the end of your neck. And that's where we're going to solve the problem.

3. *Premature ejaculation is curable—once and for all.* As soon as you *really* understand—deep inside—what your P.E. is trying to say, it will disappear. Premature ejacula-

tion is nothing more than a practical joke of the unconscious mind directed at women but, as usual, bouncing off the victim and hitting the perpetrator as well. But you know that already. In the male-female sexual arena, "minute men" are not exactly in great demand. You can put in a faster-than-lightning performance once or twice with the same partner, but then you have to start looking elsewhere.

Now let's get down to the nitty-gritty. The whole range of human sexual behavior has a powerful *symbolic* significance. So much of what you do tonight in the bedroom depends on what you did—or didn't do—a few decades ago in the nursery. Hang on now because it's going to get very interesting.

The first human experience—*and one that you never unconsciously forget*—is being fed by your mother. She takes a breast—or bottle—pushes the nipple into your mouth, and a white liquid comes squirting out. That's the first, most exciting, most important, and most unforgettable experience of your life. Not only is it vital for your survival, but it's fun. You like to drink warm milk from that stiff little nipple—everybody does. Now get ready.

Twenty-five years later the man who had a hot white liquid injected into his mouth from a stiff fleshy nipple is doing almost the same thing to a woman. This time it's a penis, not a nipple that goes into a vagina, not a mouth. The liquid is seminal fluid, not milk. But the symbolic value for the *unconscious* mind is *exactly* the same. Keep that in mind for a moment while we go back to the nursery.

What if mother didn't bring the breast or bottle to her little baby one day? The baby was aroused with hunger, aching to eat, and the hot white milk never arrived—or arrived too late to do him any good. Did it ever happen? Sure, it happened a lot. The telephone rang, another one of the kids needed something, the soup boiled over—any one of the million things that can go wrong in any household went wrong. And the little boy-baby got scared, angry, and resentful. And then when he grew up he forgot all about it—*conciously*. But the experience—*like every human experience*—remained engraved on his *unconscious* mind.

Let's swing back to the grown-up bedroom. This time the "baby"—a twenty-two-year-old, well-developed female (whom her husband may actually call "Baby")—is lying naked on the bed, just like a little baby boy used to do when he was waiting for his bottle. She too is aroused—but this time not with food hunger but with sex hunger. She too is aching to be fed—that hot white liquid from that big stiff nipple. And remember, at the moment of orgasm the vagina contracts rhythmically just like a mouth when it's swallowing milk. The nipple-penis goes into her mouth-vagina, and in ten seconds to a minute—long before she has a chance to drink it—the milk-semen is spilled. Exciting? Not for her.

It *is* exciting for the little-boy-now-grown-up who wants to get revenge for a cribside injustice that happened over twenty years ago. He still gets his kicks because now he's the mommy. That naughty baby doesn't get fed. Of course, eventually she finds someone who can and will give her the "milk" she needs, and the "milk spiller" constantly has to look for new "babies" to get revenge on.

Well, now that that's all out in the open, what do you do about it? The answer is obvious. You *stop* ejaculating prematurely. But how? Well, as we mentioned in the beginning, the goal of this book is to provide emergency emotional first aid—not in-depth psychoanalysis. (It is worth digressing a moment to mention that in-depth psychoanalysis doesn't have such a great record in curing premature ejaculation anyway.) So, without making any guarantees, here's a method of dealing with premature ejaculation that has been very successful with my patients. I hope it works for you. One more thing—you may feel silly when you're curing yourself, but you won't feel any sillier than you do when you ejaculate in the first thirty seconds of intercourse. Here goes:

1. *Before you have sexual relations think about what it all means.* Take five minutes off by yourself and remind yourself that you are *not* a bad mother who is going to spill the milk before the helpless little baby can swallow it. Sound strange? Well, it should because you are bringing the deepest functioning of the unconscious mind right out in the open. But you don't have any choice in the matter— unless, that is, you want to keep looking for girls who love getting halfway aroused and then taking a nice cold shower. As you may have noticed, there aren't too many of those around. Repeat it to yourself over and over again until it makes an impression on your unconscious *and* conscious mind. Remember, you have nothing to lose—except your premature ejaculation.

2. *From the first moment of intercourse, as soon as you get your clothes off, keep reminding yourself that you are not going to try to get revenge on your partner.* It may sound funny but keep repeating to yourself, "I won't spill the *milk,* I won't spill the *milk,* I won't spill the *milk!*" At the most critical moments in sexual intercourse, insist even harder that you're not going to "spill" your "milk." It's particularly important at the moment when you first insert your penis into the vagina, at the moment when your partner starts to get excited, and at the first hint of your impending orgasm. The best tactic is, if you feel yourself losing control, *stop, think, and repeat: "I won't spill the milk.!"*

Sound silly? You can't understand it? Your cousin who's a doctor doesn't believe in it? What do you care—*as long as it works. And it works!*

3. *Change your attitude toward women.* Along with everything else that you are doing to cure yourself, it makes sense to look at the underlying aspect of the problem of P.E. Learn to see the other half of the human

race—women—as your friends. After all, they are kind and loving creatures who can make your life happier than you ever imagined. Once upon a time you may have been a little tiny boy frightened by a great big mother, but now that's all over. For a real man a woman is not a threat, not an enemy, not a source of fear. Women are nice people, and the sooner you get used to the idea, the faster you will conquer your premature ejaculation.

# 22
## Revenge

THROUGH NO FAULT OF ITS OWN *revenge* has gotten a bad name. When you hear the word you think of a wild-eyed half-crazed creature slinking through back alleys bent on murder. From your earliest days in school you are taught that it is bad to try to get revenge. You are taught that revenge is somehow a ''dirty'' word and the best thing is to suffer in silence whatever injustice you may receive. In the Bible, in the New Testament, in the Book of Matthew, the advice is very clear: ''Whosoever shall smite thee on thy right cheek, turn to him the other also.''

Got it? If someone clobbers you on your right cheek, if you can still move your head, offer him your left cheek. Later, when you wake up in the hospital—if you ever wake up—you can try to figure out what hit you. After about three days as a human punching bag, you will have lost all your worldly possessions to muggers and be crippled for life. Should those instructions not be perfectly clear, in the same chapter, the Book of Matthew, a few lines later, there are more details:

''Love your enemies, bless them that curse you, do good to them that hate you, and pray for them which despitefully use you, and persecute you.''

Perhaps that was excellent advice in biblical times when everyone was pious and respectful(?), but in this chaotic and violent modern world that kind of counsel won't get you through twenty-four hours of contact with your fellow man.

But that's not the final word on the subject. There is another somewhat more practical point of view. It was proposed by a fellow who lived in China a few thousand years before the above words were written. His name was Confucius, and he asked the following question: *"If you reward evil with good, how do you reward good!"*

And of course, that makes sense. To be harmed and not attempt to defend yourself goes against every human—and animal—instinct. If someone does you harm, you must defend yourself. Even the tiniest ant knows that without being told. Even further, you must take steps to discourage your attacker from repeating the attack. That is the essence of survival in this difficult world. That's simple and obvious. But if it's so simple and so obvious, where does the campaign against revenge come from? That's not a hard question to answer. The campaign comes from your competition—the people and institutions who want to hold you back at the same time they are advancing themselves. They preach tolerance, patience, suffering without complaining—for you. They depict revenge as illegal, immoral and hazardous to your health.

Let's take a look at revenge and see what it really is. The word itself means "to inflict injury in return for an injury." Going back to the Holy Bible, in the Book of Exodus we find a somewhat different point of view: "And if any mischief follow, then thou shalt give life for life, eye for eye, tooth for tooth, hand for hand, foot for foot, burning for burning, wound for wound, stripe for stripe."

Interesting, isn't it? Okay, now how do we apply advice from thousands and thousands of years ago to life in the world of today? That's what Tony wanted to know.

If you had to describe Tony in one word, that word

would be "faded." He had faded blue jeans, faded tennis shoes, a faded Mickey Mouse T-shirt, and a faded outlook on life.

"I don't know, Doctor, I've never faced a problem like this one. I don't think any of my education or training has prepared me for *this!*"

"What's *this*, Tony?"

Tony sighed and leaned back in his chair.

"Ohhhh, it's a long story, but I'll give you the short version. I'm an electronics process engineer—it's a relatively new field. My specialty is microprocessor control of chemical reactions. Actually, it involves tiny computers about the size of your thumbnail that are used to control industrial processes. It's really very exciting because you can squeeze the equivalent of five hundred transistors into a space smaller than a postage stamp. Anyhow, together with a friend of mine I designed a new kind of super microprocessor.

"An ordinary one sounds pretty good. What's a '*super* microprocessor' like?"

Tony grinned.

"Well, actually, it's pretty super. The one we designed controls two hundred fourteen stages in the process of refining crude oil and replaces equipment worth about three million dollars. Our unit costs less than a hundred thousand dollars and really does a good job. That's the problem."

"Maybe I'm missing something, Tony, but I don't see the problem."

Tony scratched his head.

"It's my fault, Doctor. I get so caught up in the technical details that sometimes I lose the thread of the conversation. That's probably why I'm in this mess. As I mentioned, I developed this device with a partner. It took us four years of work and a lot of sacrifice. I think it probably wrecked my marriage too. It's hard to find a wife who's willing to sit home alone for four years while her husband solders integrated circuits all night. Well, it finally came time to sell the processor, and I found out that my partner had patented it in *his* name! He sold the first unit, took orders for tweny-two more, and kept all the money. Now he insists that all I did was help him with the details of construction. He offered me fifty thousand dollars for my share—at the rate of five thousand dollars a year. He says he's doing me a favor."

"What do you think?"

Tony leaned all the way forward in his chair and whispered: "I think he's a rotten crook! I think he's a third-rate swindler!"

"But what are you going to do about it?"

"That's my *problem!* I've been to the lawyers already, and they say I might win if I'm willing to spend five years in court and if I can come up with at least three hundred thousand dollars in legal fees. Doctor, I don't have that kind of patience or that kind of money. So, I don't know what to do."

"Are you sure you don't have any little plan in the back of your mind, Tony?"

Tony smiled a wisp of a smile.

"Well, maybe something. You see, just at the tail end of the project I discovered a glitch in the program . . ."

"A 'glitch'?"

"Sorry, Doctor, that's computer slang. A 'glitch' is a defect in a computer operation that messes everything up. In this case the glitch will let the program run fine for about a month and then . . ."

Tony broke into a wide grin.

"And then what?"

"And then it will start doing interesting things like making alcohol when you want gasoline and kerosene when you want alcohol. It might even decide to turn gasoline back into crude oil. As a matter of fact, it will operate as a random walk."

" 'Random walk'? More computer slang?"

"Sorry. That's math slang. What it means is that the microprocessor will turn on processes in a random haphazard way. It'll function like a drunk careening down the highway at ninety miles an hour. There's no way to fix it and there's no way to control it."

"Didn't you tell your ex-partner about it?"

Tony shook his head.

"I tried. But he knew it all and he wouldn't even listen to me. That was about the time my wife and I broke up, and I didn't persist. But now I don't know what to do. I don't want to get rich on this project, but I don't want to get gypped either. And my parents always taught me not to look for revenge. I just don't know what to do."

"What are you looking for, Tony?"

"What I'm looking for is just a chance to make a decent living without anyone stabbing me in the back. If I don't teach my ex-partner a lesson, he's going to keep on giving me the works. We had about a dozen other projects we were developing together, and I heard he's going to try and market those without me too. So, this is my plan. I'm perfecting the super processor and just waiting. I'm making some improvements that will let me patent it in *my* name. I'm going to let him sell the glitched version and just watch while it does its tricks. It's going to mess up those refineries so badly that I'm the only one who'll be able to set them straight. After I install my first processor all the rest will line up for their share. That's all it takes. My ex-partner will be so tied up with lawsuits that he won't even have time to plug in a soldering iron. If you call that revenge, then I'm going to get revenge."

"Tony, not only do I call that revenge, but I call that 'constructive revenge.' "

Tony nodded approvingly.

"Hmm, I like the sound of that. 'Constructive revenge.' But what does it mean?"

" 'Constructive revenge' is the literal meaning of revenge. It involves the following elements:

1. *It stops further damage to you.* The basic idea is not to start a war. The idea is to show your persecutor that it isn't worthwhile to make trouble for you. Constructive revenge finishes the problem—it doesn't start new problems.

2. *It is legal.* Blowing up your enemy's car or setting fire to his house may make you feel better for a while, but it can get you into big trouble. It's much better to use your head and put an end to the conflict once and for all.

3. *It teaches your adversary a lesson.* Even the best conceived and executed form of revenge is worthless if your adversary doesn't get the message. Make sure the message of your defensive action is unmistakable.

4. *It doesn't destroy—it creates.* Constructive revenge clears away obstacles to move ahead. It allows you to progress and to accomplish things you weren't being allowed to accomplish.''

Tony rose to leave.

''Makes sense, Doctor.''

A month later he was back. This time he was definitely *unfaded*. He sported a pair of Adidas running shoes—bright yellow. His jeans were dark blue Ultrasuede®, and his shirt was cowboy chic—blue and yellow with plenty of rivets. But it was his smile that glowed the brightest.

''How did it go, Tony?''

Bigger smile.

''Better than I expected, Doc. Two weeks after it was installed my ex-partner's processor made asphalt! It clogged all the pipes of a three hundred million dollar refinery. They're suing him for six hundred million, and he'll be in the courts for the next fifty years.''

He reached into his Gucci attaché case and pulled out a fistful of papers.

''I've got orders here for thirty-two of my own microprocessor units, and I'm in business like never before. My wife and I are going back together again—our divorce isn't final yet and we're calling it off. If that's what you call 'constructive revenge,' I'm all for it. It's punished a crook, rebuilt a business, and saved a marriage. You can't be more constructive than that!''

So, don't be afraid of revenge. Use it judiciously and with restraint, but don't hesitate to use it constructively to protect your job, your rights, and your happiness.

# 23
## Serious Illness

IN OUR MODERN SOCIETY one of the great fears of nearly everyone is a serious illness. No matter how successful you may become, no matter how famous, no matter how much money you have in the bank, if you get sick—really sick—everything you have accomplished is washed away in one frightening moment. When the doctor peers at you over the top of his or her fashionable bifocals with that very special look on his or her face, you just know that something bad is going to happen. Listen to Gerri tell about it.

Gerri is tall, thin, leggy, and strikingly beautiful. Her skin has an almost translucent appearance—as if it were lighted from inside. Her cheekbones are upswept and angular, and her hazel eyes are dramatically offset by her chestnut hair. As she speaks her voice has a seductive gentleness:

"Doctor, the word 'lucky' doesn't begin to describe me. I've been a fashion model for the past five years—ever since I was seventeen—and my life has been perfect. I earn more in one hour than the average girl makes in a week. I meet the most interesting people in the world and I love my job. I never knew what it was to worry until six months ago—but I learned fast."

"What happened, Gerri?"

"Well, just about that time I started to feel strange. In the middle of a job I'd get tremendously thirsty. I'd have to break the session to drink at least a quart of water. And then—"

"And then you developed a tremendous appetite?"

Gerri's eyes widened.

"Yes! But how did you know?"

"I'm a doctor, remember? But please go on."

"Okay. Well, I ate mountains of food. Giant sandwiches, milk shakes, french-fried potatoes, chocolate cake—everything. I was terrified that I was going to get immensely fat—but I never gained an ounce. And then I was in the bathroom all the time—urinating gallons! I finally went to the doctor and he gave me every test in the book. I'll never forget the final scene."

Gerri took out a tiny blue handkerchief and gently wiped a few tears from her eyes.

"It was just like television. My doctor sat behind this immense desk with a great big file in front of him. He acted like he was going to tell me I had three weeks to live. Then he cleared his throat and said: 'I wish I didn't have to tell you this but you have . . .'"

Gerri shuddered.

"As he was saying it all sorts of thoughts rushed through my mind. I thought it was some kind of cancer or leukemia or maybe a creeping paralysis. I started to completely lose control. All I heard was something like a voice in the distance saying one word I understood: '*diabetes.*' It was that dumb doctor telling me I had diabetes! Big deal!"

Gerri's pretty face was angry and her little fists were clenched.

"He dragged it out as if it was some terrible fatal disease and all I had was diabetes! You know, Doctor, I've always realized that my modeling work can't last forever, and I've been going to college at night for two years. I'm going to get married one of these days and have children and then I'll start to put on weight and you know how it is in modeling. If you weigh more than an underfed grasshopper, they set you to modeling shoes and gloves. Well, my major in college is, of all things, *nutrution!* So I know a lot about diabetes. It's no fun, obviously. But it's far from the end of the world. I changed my diet, I don't eat junk food anymore, and pretty soon I won't even have to take my insulin shots. But you know for a while there, I had two diseases—diabetes and stark raving terror produced by a dumb doctor.''

Gerri was smart—and courageous. And those are the two most important qualities one needs to confront any serious illness. Just as in Gerri's case, the first—and most normal—reaction is blind terror. The sudden knowledge that you are *not* immortal is unsettling in the extreme. That's what Steve found out:

''You know, I'll never forget the first night after I found out that I had Hodgkin's disease—you know, it's a form of cancer of the lymph nodes. It was just before Christmastime, and I was starting my first job as an account executive in an advertising agency. I said to myself: 'Stevie-boy, you are one dead duck! Your neck is all swollen up and you'll never see another Christmas. You are going to be very, very dead!'

''Then I started to think. Who ever promised that I was going to live forever? Who ever gave me the idea that I was even going to make it to that particular Christmas? Where was my factory guarantee of a million miles or a hundred years, whichever came first? As I lay there in bed sweating in the darkness I realized that whatever I'd been given up until then was a gift that I should be grateful for. I fell asleep and I've never really worried about it since then.''

''How long ago was that, Steve?''

Steve smiled from ear to ear.

''A mere twenty-two years ago last month, Doctor. Just twenty-two Christmases ago.''

Whenever you have to deal with a serious illness—whether it involves you personally or someone dear to you—there are some very important things you have to do right away, before you do anything else:

1. *Find out the real facts of your condition*. The days have long since passed when the doctor could justify withholding the whole truth from the patient. A patient with a potentially fatal disease has the right to know *everything* and to seek the best possible treatment—maybe even a treatment that his own doctor hasn't considered or isn't even aware of. Insist—gently but firmly—that your doctor tell you *everything* about your condition—or at least everything he knows.

2. *Don't trust any single doctor*. Doctors are only human beings—and they will be first to admit that fact. If your life and health are at stake, get the best possible opinions from the largest possible number of qualified physicians. Before a big company puts a new kind of dog food on the market, it consults a dozen experts. Your own life is at least as important as some newfangled kind of dog yummy. Doctors make mistakes—no one can deny that. And *you* don't want to be one of those mistakes. Even though it may be a little more expensive, give yourself every possible chance to come out of your condition intact. Don't try to save a few dollars here or a few dollars there. Don't carry the lab tests or X rays that one doctor has performed to the next doctor "so they don't have to be repeated." Sometimes a crucial diagnosis is made on the basis of mistaken lab tests. It is not unknown for one patient's results to get onto another patient's medical record. I will never forget the colleague of mine who treated a minister's wife for syphilis—a disease she never had. My colleague won't forget either because when she took him to court the jury decided that he had to pay her $250,000 for that careless diagnosis.

3. *Get the best treatment available*. If I could only tell

you about the patients I know of personally who are no longer here just because they didn't want to be bothered to get the best possible treatment. The temptation to have an operation at the closest hospital, to visit a clinic where it's easy to park, to take a medicine that won't upset your stomach—those are the kinds of decisions that fill cemeteries. When you have a serious illness, no matter what it is, get the *best* doctor and the *best* treatment. Don't waste time on a friendly doctor with a good bedside manner if he can't offer you the best chance of regaining your health. If you have to go to a fire-breathing dragon who sends chills up and down your spine every time you see him—but who knows how to make you well—do it!

4. *Learn, learn, learn.* It is to your advantage to learn as much as you possibly can about your disease. Don't depend on those little pamphlets you pick up in the doctor's waiting room: "Diabetes and You" and "What You Should Know About High Blood Pressure." That's fine for light reading, but when you're really sick you are involved in a fight for survival. Go to your public library and ask the librarian to help you look up all the recent magazine articles on your illness. Study them in detail until you understand *everything* they are saying about your condition. That's for openers. Then go on to the more technical articles on your disease. Ask questions of your doctor—and anyone else you can find. If your doctor doesn't want to answer your questions, maybe you need a doctor who does. Don't be put off by doctor-type reproaches like "Don't you have faith in me?" You are not going to a faith healer, you are hiring the person who has the latest and best scientific knowledge. The aim is not to make life easy for your M.D.—the aim is to make life long and healthy for *you!* You would be amazed at the number of patients who have studied their own conditions and made important contributions to their own cures. Maybe "Doctor knows best," but the patient knows something too. After all, it's *his* or *her* life that's at stake.

5. *Be prepared to sacrifice*. When you have a serious illness you have to grow up—fast. Resign yourself to do whatever is necessary to overcome your disease. If you have to stop smoking—as in the case of emphysema or Raynaud's disease—*stop smoking!* Don't cut down or taper off—*stop!* When you're dealing in terms of life or death, there's no time for being wishy-washy. If you have to stop drinking, stop *100 percent* and right away. If you have to drastically change your way of life to conquer a disease, just be grateful that there is something you can do to help yourself. If you have to lose weight, lose it— quickly and cheerfully. If you have to exercise, do it eagerly and regularly. If you have to change your diet, do it faithfully and without complaint. Once you know for sure that different habits or a different job or a totally different way of living will make you better, throw yourself into it with enthusiasm and make it work for you. Otherwise you're wasting your time and your life.

6. *Ask yourself the hardest question*. Ask yourself *"Why do I make myself sick?"* Yes, I know there are a thousand and one excuses. You can say that no one knows what makes anyone sick, that no one knows what causes cancer, and that heart disease is still poorly understood. But you know and I know that the human mind has the final say in what happens to the human body. Ask yourself this fascinating question: *"What is the purpose of my condition?"*

You may be pleasantly surprised at the answer. I say "pleasantly" because once you uncover the underlying *emotional* basis for a disease, it is often only a matter of time before the symptoms begin to clear up. Let's look at a few examples.

1. Arthritis is a disease that cripples—but it also relieves the cripple of a lot of responsibility. Haven't you noticed how often people who have to depend on their hands for a livelihood are "struck down" by arthritis? Maybe that's

the only way they can get out of working without feeling too tremendously guilty.

2. Peptic ulcers are supposed to be signs of success in the world of business. More often than not they are found in people who are consumed by ambition and competitiveness. The grim joke is that these people are literally *consumed* because their own stomach eats itself—and them!

3. A heart attack is the ultimate vacation. How often have you heard hard-driving executives say, "I know if I don't slow down, I'll have a heart attack!" And of course, they don't slow down, and of course, they have a heart attack. So often it is the only excuse workaholics can accept to justify time away from their jobs. Sometimes they get a surprise when their self-created and wished-for heart attacks take them away to another job—sitting on a cloud strumming a harp.

4. Even that most dreaded of all diseases, cancer, can have strange emotional undercurrents. Do you remember the world-famous gossip columnist who died of cancer of the *tongue?* Do you know how many women who have always felt guilty about sex develop cancer of the uterus, and almost feel relieved when they get the bad news? Do you know how many people seem to have decided to give themselves cancer and then, when a sudden change in their life occurs, decide that they don't *need* cancer after all— *and then they get well!*

The most important thing to keep in mind is that serious illness requires serious countermeasures. If you get sick, you don't have to just lie there and take it. You can fight back—in more ways than you ever imagined. As much as what your doctor does, *it's what you do that counts.* Your own efforts can easily make the difference between health and sickness, happiness and despair. It's worth remembering.

# 24
# Smoking

OH NO! Another lecture on smoking? No, certainly not. Nothing like it. We're just going to take a quick look at what smoking is all about; then we'll exit gracefully and say no more about it. The rest is up to you. As usual, you have to make up your own mind about all the important things in life.

What is this thing called "smoking" anyway? Let's take a "Man-from-Mars" peek at it and perhaps that will put it in better focus:

REPORT OF HIGH RESOLUTION RADAR OBSERVATION OF EARTH INHABITANTS . . .
DIRECTED TO: EARTH STUDY CENTER, MARS UNIVERSITY GRADUATE SCHOOL, ATTENTION EARTHOLOGY UNIT
FROM: TELERADAR UNIT ZXZ-95
SOURCE: LONG-RANGE RADAR-TELEVISION SURVEILLANCE OF EARTH INHABITANTS
DATE: 6FF PTOLMEY, 45G67H
TIME: 8:112
DETAILED ANALYSIS OF TV CASSETTES REVEALS UNEXPLAINED BEHAVIOR ON PART OF EARTHLINGS. MILLIONS OF ADULT MALES AND FEMALES OF THE SPECIES CARRY SMALL

UNITS OF THIN WHITE CYLINDRICAL OBJECTS CONCEALED IN THEIR CLOTHING OR SCATTERED AROUND THEIR DWELLINGS AND WORK PLACES. THEY HAVE BEEN OBSERVED TO PLACE THESE TUBES INTO THE OPENINGS OF THEIR LIFE-MAINTE-NANCE SYSTEMS ("RESPIRATORY TRACTS") AND THEN OXI-DIZE ("SET FIRE TO") THE TUBES AND THEIR CONTENT. THEY SUCK THE PRODUCTS OF THIS COMBUSTION ("SMOKE") DI-RECTLY INTO THEIR LUNGS.

BY MEANS OF TELE-SPECTROGRAPHY WE HAVE BEEN ABLE TO ANALYZE THE BURNED GASES WHICH THEY ABSORB AND HAVE MADE SOME AMAZING DISCOVERIES. THE GASES ARE HIGHLY TOXIC AND CONTAIN SUBSTANCES LIKE SODIUM CYANIDE, ARSENIC, NICOTINE, TAR, AND CARBON MONOX-IDE IN DANGEROUS CONCENTRATIONS. OUR OTHER OBSER-VATIONS HAVE SHOWN THESE CHEMICALS CAN PRODUCE DEATH IN EARTHLINGS. IN ADDITION, WE HAVE CONCLUSIVE EVIDENCE THAT THESE GASES PROVOKE UNCONTROLLED PRO-LIFERATION ("CANCER") IN THEIR LIFE-MAINTENANCE SYS-TEMS. WE HAVE CONSIDERED TRYING TO WARN EARTHLINGS OF THIS DANGER BUT HAVE BEEN INFORMED BY OUR TRANS-LATION TASK FORCE THAT EARTHLINGS ARE ALREADY AWARE OF ALL HAZARDS ASSOCIATED WITH THIS UNEXPLAINABLE PRACTICE! IN THE COURSE OF MONITORING THEIR COMMU-NICATIONS SYSTEMS WE HAVE ENCOUNTERED CONSTANT TRANSMISSIONS WHICH WARN THEM OF THE THREAT TO LIFE WHICH THIS CUSTOM CONSTITUTES.

WE HAVE BEEN ABLE TO OBTAIN SAMPLES OF THE SUB-STANCE WHICH THEY BURN (SOURCE: UNCLASSIFIED ALIEN PROJECT OZZXXZZO). IT CONSISTS OF FRAGMENTS OF A BROWN FERMENTED VEGETABLE LEAF COMBINED WITH VARI-OUS NOXIOUS SUBSTANCES. WE HAVE PERFORMED TELE-ELECTROENCEPHALOGRAMS TO MEASURE EARTHLING BRAIN WAVES AND HAVE FOUND NO SIGNIFICANT PLEASURE EF-FECT DURING THE PROCESS OF CONSUMING THE 'SMOKE.' FRANKLY, WE CANNOT UNDERSTAND WHAT MEANING THIS BEHAVIOR HAS FOR THEM.

WE ARE CONTINUING TO INVESTIGATE AND WILL REPORT

AGAIN IN 45T6 MEGAMINUTES. OUR CURRENT THEORY IS
THAT 'SMOKING' IS A RELIGIOUS RITUAL IN WHICH LARGE
NUMBERS OF SELECTED VICTIMS ARE SLOWLY SACRIFICED
TO APPEASE YET-UNIDENTIFIED GODS. AN IMPORTANT CLUE
SEEMS TO BE THAT NAMES AND/OR DRAWINGS OF THESE
GODS APPEAR ON THE PAPER PACKAGES THAT CONTAIN THE
WHITE LEAF-FILLED TUBES.
(SIGNED)
TELERADAR STATION ZXZ-95

Hmm, these Martians are doing a pretty good job, aren't
they? (By the way, I wonder what that ''Classified Alien
Project OZZXXZZO'' is all about? Well, maybe it's better
not to know.) Their description seems to be right on target
and well it should be since they've obviously been watching and analyzing everything we do for a long time. And
of course here on earth we all know that cigarettes are
deadly, that they do contain a long list of poisonous
chemicals, and that they obviously produce cancer in our
''life-maintenance systems.''

The only far-out part of our Martian observers' report
was their suggestion that the names and drawings on cigarette packages represented ''gods'' that the smokers worship.
That's ridiculous! *Or is it?*

Let's stop a moment and think. The truth is that almost
all cigarettes taste the same. Oh, I know, there's menthol
and mint, and strong cigarettes and mild cigarettes. But the
truth is that all cigarettes taste like cigarettes and if you
blindfold a hundred smokers and give them a dozen different brands to smoke, they won't really be able to identify
them.

And there's another interesting fact that our Martian
friends brought out: Cigarettes do not produce any measurable emotional pleasure! They produce changes in pulse
rate, strength of heart contractions, stomach secretions and
things like that, but *they do not produce any objectively
measurable physical pleasure*. Now isn't that fascinating?

But then why do people smoke? For several reasons—all of them really interesting. People smoke to *eat* a lifestyle. Does that sound weird? Well, it *is* weird. But don't take my word for it. Check the cigarette ads. Each brand is selling something—and it's not chopped-up fermented weeds wrapped in chemical-soaked paper. Look at the ads for the brand that cowboys smoke while making snarling faces from horseback. Look at the brand that emancipated women smoke while gazing smugly at the world at large. Look at the brand that young kids smoke while strolling through overgrown meadows. What the cigarette companies are telling you is that you can actually *swallow* that way of life, that set of magic fantasies, that dream trip, simply by buying and burning the little pieces of sour-smelling incense they sell. That's right, just burn the incense, smell the smoke, *swallow* the smoke, and the exciting exotic life you see in a cigarette ad is grafted onto your own humble life.

The whole business is really an extremely shrewd psychological trick taken straight from the religious beliefs of the cannibals. That's right, cannibals. In spite of what you may have heard, cannibals rarely eat their victims because they are hungry. They eat them to capture the qualities of the victims they admire the most. They generally eat the bravest enemies and the wisest intruders—which incidentally is probably the reason they ate so many foreign missionaries! But nowadays in "civilized" countries the factory worker burns the cigarette/symbol of the carefree cowboy to escape the desperate monotony of his dead-end job. The girl in the typing pool smokes the symbol of the sexually, economically, and emotionally emancipated woman to try to emancipate herself from the tedium of tapping out tedious letters. The wife who lives in a small apartment in a cold and polluted northern city smokes the cigarette that promises her a romp in a sun-filled field with an exciting young man.

But that's the problem. The cigarette-ad promise is a lie

from the start. If the factory worker wants to live a different kind of life, he has every right to do so. But eating the smoke that the "cowboy" eats won't make him the cowboy. If the secretary doesn't like her job, she should change it—and fast. But choking down the tar and nicotine that the "emancipated woman" in the ads chokes down won't give her an emancipated life. (It may well give her a ticket to the cancer ward.) If the lady in the polluted city wants clean air, she's entitled to it. But inhaling superconcentrated pollution from smoldering tobacco won't improve her life.

There's another important aspect to cigarette smoking and perhaps one that you haven't thought much about. Human beings are sucking animals. From the day of their birth they begin to suck. At first they suck a nipple, either of a breast or a baby bottle. Then they suck on candy— "suckers" to be specific. They swiftly move on to sucking on soda-pop bottles and later bottles of beer. But from a strictly psychological point of view, the most popular form of sucking is sucking on a cigarette. Why? Let's think about it.

The original liquid that humans suck is milk—a white fluid. That's their original love when it comes to sucking. Even when they don't need milk anymore, most people *want* milk. They drink it with meals, they eat it in ice cream, they suck on it in the form of *milk* chocolate. But the original way to get milk—sucking it from a breast—is now out of their reach. Or almost out of their reach. If they could just find some way to *do it without actually doing it*.

Strange as it seems, in the cigarette they discover just that way. A cigarette is white—like milk. It is tubular in shape, about the thickness of an erect well-developed female nipple. (Some cigarettes even have tips the *color* of a nipple!) It even provides about the same resistance to sucking as an actual nipple—those cigarette manufacturers have thought of everything! Even the smoke is designed to come out nice and white—just like milk. And it's not an accident that the taste of the milky smoke is faintly sweet—very much like mother's milk.

There's something else about cigarette smoking that's even more interesting. What is it that triggers the wish to smoke? Why does a smoker pick one moment and not another to light up? Let's find out. If you're a smoker, the next time you reach for a cigarette ask yourself what you were thinking about at the exact moment you felt like smoking. It's a little tricky because sometimes it's hard to keep such close track of your thoughts—they come and go so fast. But the odds are that just a moment before you felt the urge for a cigarette a thought flickered through your mind that made you feel anxious or fearful or tense. Someone said something unsettling or you heard something on the radio that triggered anxiety or you settled down for a long hard drive on a busy highway. A sip of milk translated into a suck of milky smoke from a burning cigarette calms the anxiety of the baby inside of every adult.

You don't believe me? You don't have to. Just observe your own reactions when you feel the need to smoke. If I'm right, you'll see it. And if I'm not, you'll see that too. In any event, it'll be interesting, won't it?

Well now, what do you do if you want to stop smoking? Well, what you do is simply face the reality of every smoker's situation: The truth is that only *part* of you wants to stop. The part of you that's intelligent and analytic recognizes that smoking will shorten your life, ultimately make you very sick, and cause you all kinds of problems you don't need. But the part of you that likes to guzzle smoke, likes to drink milk by proxy, loves to worship those strange little gods on the cigarette packs, wants to keep smoking *at any cost*. When the part of your mind that really wants to stop takes the upper hand, then you'll just *stop*. Taking antismoking tablets or going to stop-smoking seminars or cutting down are simply ways to make your own inner decision happen. Once you decide to stop smoking— that is, once you *really* decide to stop smoking— you'll just stop. So think about it, analyze it, and make up your own mind. After all, you're the only one who can do *that*, aren't you?

# 25
# Soft Drugs

DO YOU THINK you might have a problem with so-called soft drugs? You *think* you might but you're not sure? Let's take about thirty seconds and find out. *Honestly* answer yes or no to these six questions and we'll know the truth once and for all. *Then* we can start doing something about it. Here goes!

1. DO YOU TAKE MOOD-ALTERING DRUGS LIKE MILTOWN, VALIUM, LIBRIUM (OR ANY OF THE THOUSAND OTHER CRAZY NAMES THEY GO BY) AT LEAST THREE TIMES A WEEK—EVEN ONE LITTLE PILL A DAY?

2. DO YOU TAKE SLEEPING PILLS MORE THAN FOUR TIMES A MONTH?

3. DO YOU EVER TAKE PILLS JUST FOR FUN—THAT IS TO GET A BUZZ ON, TO TAKE A HEAD TRIP, TO FEEL GOOD?

4. WHEN LIFE HITS YOU HARD DO YOU REACH FOR YOUR PILL BOTTLE?

5. DO YOU EVER FEEL YOU JUST CAN'T GET THROUGH THE DAY WITHOUT AT LEAST ONE LITTLE PILL?

6. DO YOU EVER FEEL GUILTY ABOUT TAKING PILLS FOR DEPRESSION, ANXIETY, INSOMNIA, NERVOUS TENSION, OR ANY OTHER FORM OF EMOTIONAL DISCOMFORT?

Well, I guess I don't have to tell you. If you answered yes to *any* of those questions, you have a "soft drug" problem. The only thing is that those soft drugs aren't really so soft. Scientifically speaking, they can do you as much or more harm than the much-feared hard drugs. The proof? Here it is:

This is an excerpt from the "Warning to Doctors" about one of the most widely consumed tranquilizers; it applies equally to almost all the other prescription mind-altering drugs. As a mere patient you'll probably never see this nightmare collection of possible disasters unless of course they happen to you.

1. "Patients should avoid hazardous activities such as driving or operating machinery." So if you're going to take mind drugs, either sell your car or buy a crash helmet—and wear it!

2. "Withdrawal symptoms similar to those found in addicts to heroin and morphine have occurred in patients discontinuing this medicine abruptly. These symptoms include convulsions, vomiting and severe muscle cramps." Your doctor didn't tell you *that*, did he? As soon as you get hooked on those pills you're in the big leagues—right then and there.

3. "Adverse reactions can include hallucinations, rage, changes in libido, confusion, depression and jaundice." Did you catch that little item about "changes in libido"? That usually means that your sex drive suddenly collapses and may or may not come back. And they don't sell a pill for *that*.

You see, the problem is nobody really knows how these tremendously powerful tranquilizers work. Most of them were discovered totally by accident, and no one yet knows what the *real* hazards are. The dangers mentioned above are scary enough, but what if you take your favorite calm-down pill for the next two years and then one day your brain suddenly turns to jelly and you can't figure out which end of the toothbrush to put into your mouth? What then?

There are two very important reasons why these pills are bad for you. The first reason is physical. All these drugs are tremendously powerful chemicals which alter the basic functioning of your brain. They upset the most vital microchemical reactions, block vital nerve pathways, and distort your perception of the world around you. That's the part that few people ever stop to think about. If a threat to your survival suddenly appears, your mind and body instinctively prepare to defend you against it. That process can make you scared, alert, tense—a lot of things. But clobber your delicate brain with those pills and a garbage truck can run you over without even wiping that little smile from your lips. Even worse, once you are well tranquilized anybody can do anything they want with you.

Did you ever see those terrifying monkey movies? No? Well, that's not surprising since they generally show them only to doctors. There's this tremendously fierce monkey— all teeth and fangs—ready to rip you apart. He goes for his trainer's gloved hand and sinks those fangs in about two inches. Then they slip him a little pill—exactly the same as the tranquilizers they sell at your corner drugstore. In seven minutes flat, he's a new monkey. He sits in a corner of his cage wearing a silly grin. Then his trainer comes up and picks him up by his *tail!* The dumb monkey just grins all the more! How could that mentally castrated monkey survive the dangers of his jungle? If you take pills, how can you survive the dangers of *your* jungle?

But the second reason that pills are bad for you is the most important. *They don't change anything!* Your life can go relentlessly down the drain as you float gently by on cloud nine. You drift along in your tranquilizer cocoon as job, friends, and future all slowly ooze away. Not only do mind-altering prescription drugs change the way your brain functions *physically*, they gradually deprive you of your hard-won mechanisms of defense. Every trick you have learned over the years goes up in smoke as soon as the pill hits your head. Suddenly, for the next four hours, you're as helpless as a baby. By the fifth hour you're starting to recover—unless you take another pill. That's a bigger problem than many people ever realize. Once you start on the pills you're putty in the hands of others. A manipulating wife, a domineering husband, a boss who loves to exploit his employees—they *love* to have their victim on tranquilizers. So if you want to be in charge of your own destiny, flush those little brain-blasters down the toilet—but in the right way at the right time, as we'll see in a moment.

Well, you really knew all that, didn't you? Sure. But the big question is *how* to stop, how to get off those pills once and for all. There are two ways. The first way is the way *not* to do it. Don't stop cold turkey. As the drug companies warned your doctor—and as they *should have* warned you—kicking your tranquilizers all of a sudden may dump you into a withdrawal syndrome just like those you've seen in the movies—only worse. If you are taking tranquilizers or antidepressants, use the "Eight Days and Away" technique. This is how it works:

If you're taking three pills a day, keep ten of those little monsters and throw all the rest away! Right now! Today take three pills, as usual. Tomorrow take two pills, and take two pills the next day. Then take one a day for two days, and then take no pills at all on the sixth day. The seventh day take one pill, and the eighth day, you're home free—nothing! Here it is in diagrammatic form:

| DAY | | | | | | | |
|---|---|---|---|---|---|---|---|
| 1 | 2 | 3 | 4 | 5 | 6 | 7 | 8 |

| PILLS | | | | | | | |
|---|---|---|---|---|---|---|---|
| 3 | 2 | 2 | 1 | 1 | 0 | 1 | 0 |

If you've been taking four pills a day, just follow the same routine: four pills the first day, then three, three, two, two, one, one, none, one, none.

If you've been taking sleeping pills, the way out from under is a little different. There are two basic types of sleeping pills in common use. First, there are the barbiturates. These are common chemical poisons, which literally snuff out the most important areas of the brain one by one. If you take a big enough dose, they will kill you. And people *do* kill themselves by a simple overdose of barbiturates. If you're taking them, the best way out is just to *stop*—that's it. Your first night off the pills may be a little wakeful—but maybe not. You may be pleasantly surprised. In any event, schedule your stopping for a time when you don't have to be at your best the next day. The second night you may be surprised to sleep better than you expected. You can help get rid of the residues of barbiturates that build up in your body by drinking plenty of liquids and getting plenty of exercise. Walking, biking, jogging, swimming—anything you like to get the juices flowing—will help tremendously.

If you're taking another kind of sleep medicine—of the tranquilizer family or the antihistamine family—it's best to taper off to avoid unpleasant surprises. You've become a type of addict to that stuff, and you have to come down slowly. Take your regular dose tonight, half of that tomorrow night, and half of that the next night. Then get ready for a little tossing and turning the following night. (It may *never* happen.) Then you're off that bad stuff once and for all.

Final questions? How do you sleep without pills? How do you function without tranquilizers? The precise answers are to be found in Chapter 5, Anxiety, Chapter 10, Depression, Chapter 17, Insomnia, and Chapter 18, Loneliness. But before you turn to those chapters, think about it this way. When you take tranquilizers and other mind-benders, you have *two* problems: your original problem *plus* the relentless and very real damage that the drugs are doing to your mind. The moment you kick the pills you've reduced your real-life problems by at least 50 percent. And that's not bad! There's no reason in the world not to do it; no normal person who has gotten away from the pills has ever wanted to go back. So you know what you have to do—and good luck!

# 26
# Suicide

YOU FEEL LIKE KILLING YOURSELF? All right. But before you do take a couple of minutes to read this chapter.
If you still feel like doing yourself in after that, that's up to
you. But there are a couple of things you should consider
first.

To start off with, *you* didn't decide to kill yourself. That
decision was made for you by forces within your mind that
you don't control and probably are not even aware of. In a
sense it's the result of a battle that occurred inside your
head—a battle that you lost without even knowing that it
took place! All you got was a little telegram saying:
"SITUATION IMPOSSIBLE. YOU ARE BETTER OFF DEAD. PRO-
CEED TO ELIMINATE YOURSELF IMMEDIATELY! END OF
MESSAGE"

Just think about it a moment and you'll realize it's true.
The impulse to murder yourself pops up when all the
emotional doors slam shut. Ordinarily in life you can
choose from several solutions to every problem that con-
fronts you. For example, if you don't like your job, you
can quit; you can move to another city; you can start your
own business; you can join the army; you can enter a
commune—you can move relatively easily from one level

201

of existence to another. But sometimes destiny seems to deal you a set of cards that can be played only one way—by knocking yourself off. *Or at least that's the way it seems.* In reality, it's only another trick that your mind plays on you. *Suicide is always presented to the victim as the only way out! In every case there are at least three other alternatives that the person has failed to consider!*

You want the proof? Okay, consider this example:

One of the most frequent reasons for attempted suicide, especially in women, is unhappy love affairs. Donna is a typical case.

Because Donna is a bright attractive brunette in her middle twenties, it's hard to believe that she could have been on the brink of assassinating herself:

"I can't believe it was only three months ago that I was ready to kill myself, Doctor. It seems like a nightmare!"

"It *was* a nightmare, wasn't it, Donna?"

"What do you mean?"

"I mean, you were going around in a daze, out of contact with reality, alone and terrified."

Donna sighed.

"That's for sure! You know the story. I'd been living with Kent for about two years, and we were going to get married in a few weeks. I was two months pregnant and really looking forward to a great new life. I'll never forget that cold wet November afternoon. I was struggling with one of those pregnancy depressions, and it had been a terrible day. I came back from shopping, opened the door to our apartment, and everything was gone! I mean, the sofa, the rugs, our bed, the stove, even the bathroom towels. That rat sold everything, cleaned out our bank account, and just disappeared. That afternoon, the moment I turned the doorknob, the whole world fell in on me!"

And that's the way it is. When reality presses down on you with a force of about ten tons, a little voice inside your head delivers the suicide telegram. But you don't have to accept it. You can *analyze* your situation, *understand* it, and *overcome* it. Here's how.

Every person who contemplates suicide is a victim of the same basic accusations from his or her *inner enemy*. Everyone is accused of the same basic offenses:

1. *You are stupid.* You allowed yourself to be exploited and massively mistreated.

2. *Everyone is laughing at you.* You made a fool of yourself and everyone knows it.

3. *There is no other alternative—you are better off dead.* If you continue living, your existence will be unbearable.

4. *Somebody clobbered you and you have no way to fight back.* You were wronged and there is no way you can defend yourself.

These were the accusations against Donna, and they are virtually the same in every case. The last accusation is particularly interesting because in every suicide there is an element of *murder*. Every person who kills himself or herself is, at the same time, murdering someone else by proxy. In Donna's case she wanted to *symbolically* kill Kent, the man who monopolized two years of her life, made her pregnant, promised to marry her, and then deserted her. The simultaneous accusations of *stupidity, ridicule, no way out, and no possibility of revenge* overwhelm the emotional defenses of the human organism and trigger the suicide telegram. Okay, now that you understand that, what do you do?

You defend yourself, of course. The first thing you do is take certain emergency measures. Your life is in danger: Somebody wants to kill you, and the fact that it's *you* means you have to act doubly fast. The first step is to shift the balance of power from your inner forces to your outer forces—from the *unconscious mind* to the *conscious mind*. You have to take *conscious* control over what's happening.

Decrease your vulnerability by taking these emergency measures immediately:

1. *Don't drink—at all!* Alcohol strengthens your destructive forces and weakens your ability to save yourself.

2. *Don't take pills.* You don't need to be tranquilized, dazed, doped, or anything else. You need a crystal-clear mind to fight your way out of a tough spot.

3. *Don't watch television or go to the movies.* If that sounds funny, just analyze it a moment. In both cases you will be sitting immobile in semidarkness while scenes of violence and emotional conflict are pumped into your mind. Both TV and movies wallow in death, sadism, depression, and defeat; that's what you're trying to avoid, remember?

4. *Get out of your house.* When you are trapped indoors you get the mistaken idea that the whole world is closing in on you. That's not true, of course, but you have to be outside in the open air to realize it.

5. *Put yourself in contact with other people.* Plain old friendly people will do. Don't go to bars. Don't haunt places where you have suffered before. Find basic human contacts at the simplest possible level—to answer back the internal accusations that there is no one to talk to or nothing to do about your situation.

Once you have taken these five emergency measures you can go on to the next step. *You can use your destructive impulses to destroy the inner forces that are threatening you.* If you want to kill something, don't kill yourself. Kill the elements *within your own mind* that are your real enemies. Consider these *facts:*

1. *There is no reason to throw yourself away as if you were a bag of garbage.* You don't have to waste your life; you can spend it. If your life isn't worth anything to you, you can at least make it work for someone else. Go to work in a hospital for crippled children or an orphanage. Sign up for the Peace Corps or the Foreign Legion or as a

missionary worker in Africa. As long as you don't care what happens to you, make your life work to benefit someone else.

2. *You can buy yourself breathing space.* Step out of your present life for a few months. Put your entire existence on hold. There are a few simple ways to do that. You can enter a monastery or a convent—not as a priest or as a nun but as a "guest." Your life will be simple, secure and tranquil. You will also find the time to analyze your problems and realize that suicide is a dumb solution for dumb people. Sometimes a commune, carefully selected, can serve the same purpose.

3. *Climb aboard a spaceship.* Transport yourself to a different world where the problems that seem immense to you are of absolutely no importance to the people there. In Sandusky, Ohio, everyone may know about your disgrace. But in Tarpon Springs, Florida, you're a new person. Sometimes you have to go farther. Maybe Australia or Brazil will provide the atmosphere of a "new planet" that you need to put things in perspective. Don't hesitate to take what may seem to be drastic measures to save your life—it's worth it!

There's another aspect that we have to face honestly as well. These days, the United States is not the warmest and friendliest place in the world—especially for someone who is depressed. It's hard to meet people when you need them the most, and sometimes everyone seems to live in their own closed little circle. And when you're really feeling bad it's more difficult than ever to break into tight little groups. Latin countries like Spain, Italy, Mexico, and the other countries of Latin America are far warmer and more open. In addition, when it's cold and cloudy where you are, it is usually warm and sunny there. It's much harder to be depressed on the beach when the sun is shining. Sometimes just a little trip in that direction will give you an entirely new perspective. It might be worth a try.

4. *Think of the other end of the tunnel.* Everyone in this

world has their bad moments. We all have to go through difficult, dangerous and distasteful situations. We all have to pass through the darkest of tunnels. But every tunnel has a way out at the other end. It's worthwhile to keep this clearly in mind while you're taking all the other measures to defend yourself. What may have seemed to be the greatest threat to your survival a few years ago in retrospect now looks like only a bump in the road. The immense crisis you face today will amount, six months from now, to a minor nuisance.

5. *Be tough.* When you come right down to it, your survival depends on your ability to confront and overcome the hazards of your daily existence. Donna put it this way:

"You know how hard it was for me, Doctor, after Kent ran out on me. I was alone, sick, desperate and destitute—and pregnant. I was more than willing to kill myself. Well, I did everything that you told me to do, and it pulled me through—fast. But I think one of the things that you explained to me helped me more than anything. I hated Kent, that's true, and one of the basic reasons I didn't kill myself is that *I didn't want to give him the satisfaction!*"

Don't kill yourself. Don't give *anybody* the satisfaction.

# 27
# Unemployment

"UNEMPLOYED!" *"Out of work!"* *"No help wanted!"*
What's that all about? Crowd scenes from a movie about
the Great Depression? No sir, that's the world of today.
Suddenly, without any good reason, the nightmare threat
of *no job* and *no income* circles like a vulture over tens of
millions of hardworking Americans. And to millions more
it's more than just a threat—it's a reality. Listen to Fred:

"You know, my dad always used to talk about the
Depression, and I never really understood what he meant.
After all, I'm only forty, so I was born after it was all
over. But now I know."

Fred scratched his head.

"You know, Doctor, I thought I had it made. And I
did—until about three months ago. I'm a design engineer
in the automobile industry. My specialty is the greenhouse—
you know what that is?"

Without waiting for an answer, Fred went on.

"It's the part of the body above the fenders—the roof
line, the windows, all that. It's actually the most important
part of the car, style-wise. That's where we try to sneak in
a hint of Mercedes or Rolls-Royce into our four-cylinder
rust-mobiles. Maybe that's not one hundred percent right,

but I guess I'm a little bitter. I worked for that company fifteen years, and the minute business fell off, they put me out in the street.''

Fred's jaw tightened.

''Imagine! I was pulling down thirty-five thousand dollars a year. I had a big mortgage on my house, payments on two cars, and about sixteen thousand dollars in assorted bills to pay—you know, credit cards and all that. They just pulled the rug out from under me!''

''What are you going to do?''

Fred's eyes widened.

*''Do? Do?* What do you think I'm going to *do?* There's not a damn thing I *can* do! I gave fifteen years of my life to that damn company, and as soon as things slowed down they canned me! I've lost my house and one of my cars, and tomorrow I'm going to see the lawyer about filing for bankruptcy. They never gave me a chance!''

''But haven't you tried to find another job?''

Fred half-leaped out of his chair.

''Another job? How many jobs do you think there are for unemployed designers of car roofs? There aren't six companies in the United States that make cars, and most of them are on the brink of disaster. Who's going to give me a job?''

''Well, what else can you do?''

Fred sank back into his chair. His voice was low and subdued.

''Wash windows? Pump gas? Sell life insurance? People are washing their own windows. If they can't sell cars, how can they sell gas? People are cashing in their life insurance. I don't know what to do.''

A familiar story? Perhaps. And it's interesting in more ways than one. Fred made every mistake in the book when it came to facing the specter of unemployment. Let's list some of those mistakes.

1. *He didn't understand the economics of employment.* He crippled himself emotionally by getting angry with the

company that fired him. He talked about "giving fifteen years of my life" to an ungrateful business enterprise. What Fred couldn't face was that his ex-employer was just as much a machine as the machine that stamped out the "greenhouses" of the cars he used to design. The company paid him for his labor only as long as it could make a profit on him. When he was no longer profitable to the company, it discarded him. It didn't know—and it didn't want to know—about his mortgage, his children, or his problems.

2. *He forgot about the deal he made.* By accepting the supposed security of a fixed salary, he exposed himself to the risk of being fired whenever his bosses felt like firing him. *Whenever you accept a job you must accept the risk of having that job taken away from you.* Everyone from the president of the company to the man who sweeps the floors can be out of a job from one day to the next.

3. *He never made alternative plans.* He never faced the fact that the job market is a battlefield. The conflict is between the employee who wants to sell his skills—such as they are—at the highest possible price and the employer – who wants to pay the lowest rate for the most work. Fred gravitated into a highly specialized line of work—roof design of automobiles—and wasn't ready when his employer decided to do without him. In the course of one hour he fell from a high-level complex job with little competition to the lowest level of all—no skills, no *transferable* experience, and millions of men competing at the same level. Washing windows, pumping gas, selling insurance—that's the bottom of the barrel when it comes to working.

4. *He reacted emotionally.* Earning a living is a complex struggle for survival—it is not a tea party. The world of private enterprise is a jungle with no room for emotion. If you are trapped in the jungle and a tiger chases you, do you respond by delivering a lecture to the tiger on the injustice of eating poor little human beings? I don't think

so. I think you run as fast as you can and get yourself away from that tiger. Private enterprise has one goal: *making money*. Anyone who interferes with that goal gets steamrollered. Fred didn't do anything bad—he simply had become a liability in his bosses' program to make money. He has to accept that fact just as coldly as his bosses do. It might help to realize that the big shots of commerce and industry fire each other with the same coldness and inhumanity. When one company takes over another, there can be a "massacre of vice-presidents." The man who held the reins of power can suddenly find himself . . . but wait, Roger tells it better.

"I tell you, it was quite a morning!"

"What do you mean, Roger?"

"That's what happened when my company gave me a new office, Doctor. Looking back on it, it was really funny, but at the time it was superweird, I'll tell you that! It happened about six months ago. I was home having breakfast with my wife one morning about seven-thirty when there was a knock on the door. I hardly heard it because I was thinking about the deal I had going. I was senior vice-president of a microelectronics outfit at the time, and we had a big contract going down. I had a meeting scheduled at eleven that morning to put on the finishing touches. It was going to be my best shot. I was making . . ."

Roger stopped to think.

"Let's see, about one hundred sixty thousand dollars a year plus pension and profit sharing and bonus and stock options—say two hundred thou. Anyhow, Joyce went to the door, and when she came back into the kitchen she was a little pale. She said there were two fellows at the door who wanted to see me, dressed in business suits. To be honest, the first thing I thought of was the tax guys—you know, the IRS. But they don't usually get up that early. I gulped down my coffee and went to the door to talk to them, and boy, it was really freaky."

Roger unzipped his thin nylon jacket and leaned back in his chair.

"There were two of them all right—a fat kid and a thin weasely guy, about forty-five. They both looked like safecrackers. Fatty had a cardboard carton under his arm. When I got to the door, the Weasel pulled out a badge—it said '*Private Investigator*.' He asked me if I was me, and then the fatso shoved the carton at me. I opened it up and it had all the stuff from my desk! You know, pens, calendars, pictures of the kids. Then they gave me a two-line letter from the chairman of the board of our great company telling me I was canned as of that moment. Stapled to it was a check for two weeks pay. Then Skinny told me not to try to come back to the office."

Roger smiled.

"I asked him if it was all right to stop by once in a while to beg for alms in the parking lot. He didn't like my little joke, and he took a couple of steps toward me."

"What did you do?"

Roger looked surprised.

"What did I do? I told him he had about two seconds to get off my front porch or I'd pop him one!"

"What did he do?"

"What would *you* do? He got off my front porch!"

Roger laughed.

"But what was that you said about a new office?"

"Oh yeah. Well, you should have seen my office at *corporate headquarters*. Eight hundred square feet of executive privilege. Carpets up to your knees, two windows, a computer terminal, a Telex, and *two* genuinely awful oil paintings. They took all that away from me. But I have a new office now, and I like it even better. It's ultramodern— all shiny chrome and glass with four picture windows and a panoramic view. It's so crammed with communications gear that I can hardly sit down, but it gives me a direct line to anywhere in the world."

"Roger!"

Roger winked.

"Okay, Doc. It's just my sense of humor. So I'm working out of a phone booth! For the first time in twenty years, I'm my own boss. As soon as I got fired I sat down with Joyce—that very morning—and we took stock of the situation. I'm not a spring chicken anymore—I'm fifty-six—so I have to face reality. I know those corporate geniuses aren't combing the streets for a fifty-six-year-old unemployed vice-president. I had about ten thousand in the bank and a house that was paid for. We decided to rent the house for nine hundred dollars a month and move to an apartment. That runs us about two hundred seventy-five dollars. I know—it's a small place. That's why I made my calls from the phone booth. I didn't want Joyce to suffer with me when I got turned down."

"Did you get turned down?"

Roger shrugged.

"Only about four hundred times. Listen, vice-presidents are a dime a dozen. It's a title on the door—nothing else. I like the title on the door of my new office much better. It says 'Telephone.' It has nice big letters all in blue, and at least it's honest. So after about three weeks of getting the bum's rush, I sat down again with Joyce to plan my next move."

Roger sighed.

"I tell you, Doctor, I couldn't have made it without that girl. Anyhow, we started talking, and after about two hours we came to the conclusion that I wasn't the only one with economic problems. A lot of office people that were still working were hurt by inflation and budget cuts. That's how the idea was born."

"What idea?"

"Why, 'Park-A-Pizza,' Doctor! Haven't you tried one? Seriously, what we decided to do was make some miniature pizzas—just enough for one person—and load up my station wagon with them. There's a big office center about six blocks from our new apartment—not far from my phone booth. I hit the parking lot about noon, and the first day I sold about six pizzas, but I didn't worry. They were cheap and good. You know, cheese and peppers. The next day the word started to get around, and I moved two dozen. Now I sell two hundred a day there, and I have five new lots that I'm starting to service. I also make them for parties, and we're starting a take-out place next week. It won't be long before we're earning enough to move back into our old house. And you know what?''

There was a twinkle in Roger's eye, and I could sense what was coming next.

"Okay, sock it to me, Roger."

"The most fun is the last stop on my route. It's the parking lot of the complex where I used to work. Boy, is it fun to sell pizzas to my former colleagues. I sit on the tailgate of my station wagon passing out pizzas and taking in the money, and those poor guys come out in their Countess Mara ties and their Gucci loafers. They stare at me in my Tiawan twelve ninety-five corduroys and my Korean tennis shoes, and I can see the envy in their eyes. They chomp their pizzas and creep back to their offices, and I spin down the road in my pizza wagon, free as a bird!''

What did Roger do right? Almost everything. Let's make another list.

1. *He reacted without emotion.* Except for shock and surprise at the hateful way he was fired, he kept his cool. His years of experience in the corporate desert helped him realize that he couldn't expect anything from his former bosses. He then proceeded to analyze coolly his assets and liabilities and make the best of them.

2. *He immediately tried to get a job in his area of greatest experience.* That was the reason behind the four hundred telephone calls. He got in touch with anyone he could think of in any area remotely related to what he knew and offered his services. He sent out résumés to

every possible employer. He wisely took himself out of his house so he could work independently without upsetting his family. (His story about the telephone booth was true.)

3. *He wasn't afraid to lower his standard of living.* It was no fun to move out of a big house in a fashionable neighborhood and rent a tiny apartment on the edge of a commercial district. What he didn't mention was that he sold his new Volvo and his wife sold her Ford. He stopped playing golf, and his wife gave up her luncheon club. They stopped going out to eat once a week. She started to make her own clothes. They did everything possible to economize. He cut his expenses to the bone because he really didn't know how he was going to earn his living.

4. *He kept his sense of humor.* Losing your job is not the end of the world—unless you convince yourself that it is. Roger rolled with the punches. When he saw that he wasn't going to get back into the executive orbit, he came up with a new idea, rolled up his sleeves, and made it work.

5. *He wasn't afraid of hard work.* He got up at 3:00 A.M. to roll out the pizza dough and bake the pizzas. He was at the wholesale market buying supplies by six. Then he spent the morning setting up new routes and calling on caterers for party sales. He started for the parking lots by eleven and sold until one thirty. Then he collected from his other salesmen and did accounts until three thirty in the afternoon. He worked harder for himself than he ever worked for his former bosses, and he earned more in pride and freedom—if not in money.

Anybody can follow Roger's example. You may not end up selling pizzas in parking lots, but there is *something* you can do to earn your living anywhere you find yourself and under any set of circumstances. And anybody can follow Fred's example. There are plenty of people sitting in front of their television sets collecting unemployment compensation and feeling sorry for themselves. The difference between them boils down to the difference between *easy-hard* and *hard-easy*. What Fred is doing—self-pity and passivity—is *easy* now, but it's going to get very *hard* later on. Roger's way was *hard* at first, but now it's very, very *easy*. The choice? As usual, it's all up to you!

# 28
# Unhappy Love Affairs

HOW DOES THAT SAYING GO? "Lucky in cards, unlucky in love"? Well, there must be millions of people who are *very lucky* in cards. Just glance around and you can see an awful lot of people who seem to be not only *unlucky* but also *unhappy* in love. And if you can't see them, you can hear them. In those great mirrors of human emotions—television, movies, and popular songs—there seems to be only one kind of love—the *unhappy* kind. Every love story starts off with a bang, but they all seem to end in 3-D—disappointment, disillusion and dismay. Even if a love affair should end in its logical conclusion, marriage, in many cases it doesn't seem to make a difference. How does it go? "What are the three rings in marriage?" Answer: "The engagement ring, the wedding ring, and suffering."

It's just as puzzling to Suzanne. She is twenty-five, slender, and very pretty. But that doesn't always help:

"Doctor, I've been in love at least three times this year—and it's only August! But that doesn't mean I know any more about what love is than I did last year at this time."

She shook her honey blond curls.

216

"As a matter of fact, instead of an answer, I have a question: 'If love is so good, how come it makes me feel so bad?' "

"I think I can answer that, Suzanne, but let me ask you a couple of questions first. How do your love affairs start out?"

Suzanne smiled—and displayed a row of perfect dazzling teeth.

"I can answer that pretty well. I just fell in love again last month! You know, what can I say? I meet a man and I like him. We start talking and it's obvious that he likes me too. He's interesting and exciting and I just feel good all over. He usually takes me to super places—you know, little 'in' restaurants and very special little nooks—and it's like walking on air. We do a lot of talking. I tell him my life story and he tells me his life story, and then of course we get down to sex.

"And how does that go?"

She rolled her pale green eyes upward.

"Just like everything else—great! I should say, great at first! Because just like everything else, it starts to wear off. I mean, the conversation is super, the weekends are exciting, the orgasms are sensational, but slowly we both come down to earth."

"What do you mean, 'come down to earth'?"

Suzanne wrinkled her pert little nose.

"Well, you know. Every boyfriend has only so many funny little stories to tell. I can almost make a list of the ones I've heard. There's the 'what I did in the war' story. There's the 'I got so drunk I didn't know what I was doing' story. There's the 'what I really want out of life' story."

Suzanne shivered.

"Then there's the 'I never met a girl like you before' story. Sometimes I feel like I've heard all their material before. By the time they get down to the 'nobody understands me' stories, I want out. It always seems to end the same way! In the beginning I can't *stand* to be away from them and in the end I can't *wait* to get away from them! But at least I'm smarter than my girl friends!''

''In what way?''

''Well, I don't get married to them! I find out they're not for me long before I burn any bridges.''

''But aren't you a little cynical about this whole business. Suzanne? Excuse me for saying this, but you seem to look down on these former boyfriends of yours. It's as if they deliberately set out to do you harm.''

Suzanne shook her head vigorously.

''Nothing could be farther from the truth, Doctor. You know, I'm not exactly a child anymore. I have my master's degree in sociology, and my specialty is Human Resources. I'm as well aware as anyone of the limitations of human beings. But all my theoretical knowledge doesn't seem to translate into happiness for myself. I may be pretty but I'm not dumb!''

''I'm sure you're right on both counts. Why don't you describe, in detail if you can, what went wrong the last time you fell in love.''

''Sure. That would be Kim. Well, I met Kim at a seminar for sociologists. He's a clinical psychologist in private practice—he has his own clinic. He's thirty-four, been married once, divorced once, and drives an Astin-Martin. He looks like Clark Gable used to look, and he's into jogging, macrobiotic diets and photography. He lives in this great condominium right on the beach, and he has his own sailboat.''

''What else can you tell me about him, Suzanne?''

She thought a moment.

''Well, he dresses great. You know, nice clothes but not too flashy. Oh yes, he has a motorcycle. A BMW R-sixty-five, if you know what that is.''

''Yes I know what it is. But how is Kim as a *person?*''

''Oh yes. Well he has some funny ideas about sex. I mean, he's big on amyl nitrite and things like that. I don't especially care for that sort of thing. I like my sex straight, if you know what I mean.''

''Sure, I know what you mean. Are you ready for the answer to your question?''

Suzanne nodded eagerly.

''That's why I'm here, Doctor!''

''Okay. Here we go. I asked you to describe Kim. But you didn't describe him. What you described instead was a series of full-page ads from a macho men's magazine. It's fascinating to know that he owns a BMW R-sixty-five motorcycle, has a fashionable condo at the beach, drives an Aston-Martin, eats a macrobiotic diet, jogs, takes pictures, and sniffs amyl nitrite to prolong his orgasms. But how is he as a *human being?*''

Suzanne didn't answer for at least half a minute.

''Maybe you're on to something, Doctor.''

''Maybe I am. What do you two talk about?''

She ran her fingers through her hair nervously.

''You mean what did we *use* to talk about. We broke up last week. Actually, I talked mostly about myself—what I wanted. And he talked mostly about himself—how nobody understood him and how his patients didn't really appreciate all he was doing for them. I guess we just got bored with each other, that was all.''

''Okay, Suzanne, let's get down to basics. The reason that two people fall in love with each other in the beginning has a lot to do with the tremendous amount of emotional energy that is part of everyone's personality. All this emotional energy that's pulsing around in your mind and body can be invested in someone else. It's like plugging all the energy of your personality into someone else's personality. Your energy flows into him and his energy flows into you. That's why, in the beginning, when you first make contact with a new boyfriend, everything is so great. That personal energy flows back and forth in tremendous surges. His flows toward you and yours flows toward him—almost like bolts of lightning. Sex has a lot to do with that energy, and that's the reason why sex is so great for both of you in the beginning. Are you with me so far?''

"With you? I'm ahead of you! This is fascinating!"

"Okay, hang on. It's gets better! Obviously, you can't just plug your personality into any man that strolls by your door. You need someone that you can *identify* with. That simply means that he has a certain number of individual characteristics that correspond to your personality. For example, you'd find it hard to fall in love with a sixty-year-old man who was five feet tall, only spoke Hungarian, and had a secondhand store in Cleveland.''

Suzanna laughed—nervously.

"I'd have to agree with you. Cleveland! Imagine! Cleveland of all places!''

"But you see, that's the problem. I didn't pick those characteristics at random. Of all the qualities of that mythical boyfriend, the one that disqualifies him the *least* is the place he lives. But that's the one that repels you the most. Really the most significant for you—a twenty-five-year-old English-speaking woman—is his age, sixty, his sole language, Hungarian, and maybe his occupation, used merchandise. Cleveland is beside the point.''

Suzanne seemed transfixed.

"Now, let's apply that to Kim. You plugged into him on the basis of the *superficial qualities* that you identified very early in the game . . .''

Suzanne interrupted.

"You mean his Aston-Martin and his pad on the beach and his macro diet?''

"Right. And his occupation—psychologist—and his clothes—'nice but not flashy.' But he could be a plastic bionic man—manufactured to order. You know, 'Send me up a divorced-psychologist pattern, Gable type, macro-jogger, beach, with sailboat and motorcycle modules. Make it the light-duty model—it only has to last a month!''

"But how did I *know* all those things, Doctor?''

"Stay with me and you'll see. There's an interesting psychological phenomenon called 'imprinting.' You must be familiar with it."

"Sure. It's the engraving of complete patterns from the outside world onto the human mind."

"That's right. Well, like it or not, Suzanne, you've been imprinted. From your years of watching TV and going to the movies and reading magazines and newspapers, you have an almost indelible pattern of the 'ideal man' imprinted on your brain. A lot of it is unconscious, but plenty of it is conscious as well. Let me describe it to you and tell me if it fits. Okay?"

"You bet! I'm dying to hear it!"

"Fine. Your ideal man is tall, not short. He is slim, not fat. His nose is small; his jaw is square; his eyes are set wide apart in his head. He has square shoulders; he doesn't wear glasses, and he has muscles. His clothes are snug but not tight, and he has a suntan but his skin is not too dark. He is not specifically ethnic. That is, he is not a Negro or an Oriental. He is not specifically Italian or Mexican. Am I on the right track?"

"Too close for comfort, Doctor."

"Okay. He is prosperous although not wealthy, and he is not a blue-collar worker. He isn't a plumber or a carpenter. He is ideally in one of the professions—psychologist, medical doctor, architect, something like that. His interests are 'fashionable' interests. If jogging is in, he's a jogger. If sailing is in, he's a sailor. He is smart but not too intellectual. He flaunts the 'big boys' toys like motorcycles, sailboats, sports cars, videotape recorders, stereos and all the rest. Does that fit Kim?"

"Kim? It fits every man I ever went with! But what's wrong with going with men like that?"

"There's nothing wrong with it unless you mind trading them in every couple of months. Didn't you notice, Suzanne? *Not one of the qualities I just listed had anything to do with being a desirable human being.* The shape of his jaw?

The fit of his pants? His suntan? What you have been looking for—and finding—isn't a person but a *screen.*"

Suzanne's voice rose right up the scale.

"A screen? What do you mean?"

"Just that. You were looking for someone that was all surface—just like a movie screen. A nice thin surface so you could project your own personality right onto him. You didn't want any real human qualities to get in the way. For example, part of what you try to project as part of your own personality is 'coolness' or lack of emotion.'"

"Lack of emotion? I resent that!"

"I thought you would. But just look at the cold hateful way you were describing your past boyfriends. 'Funny little stories' and 'I've heard all their material.' And of course, that's the problem. All that emotional energy that you should be plugging into your boyfriends never penetrates beneath the surface—because there's nothing to penetrate into. And they can't really plug into you because you make yourself just as superficial in relation to them. Both of you spend most of your time acting out something you have absorbed from the movies or TV, but since those electronic love stories only skim the surface, you've never learned what to do next—after the movie is over.'"

A frown creased that pretty little forehead.

"Can you be more specific, Doctor?"

"Sure. Those hundreds of movies you've seen take you right through the preliminaries: boy meets girl. Boy talks to girl. Boy gets into bed with girl. Boy gets out of bed with girl. *The end!* Lights go on in the movie theater. Deodorant commercial runs on TV. You don't know what happens after that, and maybe you don't *want* to know what happens after that.'"

"Why shouldn't I want to know?"

"Maybe you're scared to find out."

"Maybe I am. Keep going."

"Right. So, you're a flat little screen and your boyfriend is a flat little screen, and you flash your little script on him and he flashes his little script on you. Nothing penetrates. You don't *absorb* anything from him and he doesn't *absorb* anything from you. That's why he has to use drugs during sex and that's why you have to use drugs—at least sometimes."

"I'm not admitting anything."

"You don't have to. But you're not denying it, are you?"

Suzanne blushed a deep shade of pink.

"No, I'm not denying it. But I *want* to feel something."

"That's exactly what I was telling you. Incidentally, that's the reason most people do drugs—they're desperate to at least feel *something*. I'm sure you can see why you fall in and out of love so frequently. The men in your life are so shallow you can't fall very deep. After all, a movie only runs ninety minutes."

"But what about all those bad scenes?"

"What bad scenes do you mean?"

"You know, before we break up. Like Kim last week. He said I was a stupid superficial little girl. He called me 'immature' and 'materialistic' and 'egotistical.' He said all I was interested in was the latest hairdo and not in anyone else."

"What did you say to him?"

"I was afraid you'd ask, Doctor. I told him he was more in love with himself than anyone else and that he used people like paper napkins. Once they served their purpose he just discarded them. I also told him he had a good mind but he never gave it any exercise. It was really a horrible scene! But why?"

"That's an easy one. It was a horrible scene because both of you were telling the truth—but not the way you intended. Kim thought he was describing *your* defects but he was actually listing his *own*. Look, he called you 'immature, materialistic, egotistical.' Isn't that Kim?"

"Whew! That's scary! Sure that's Kim. And 'interested in the latest hairdo'? He spends thirty dollars every two weeks to have *his* hair styled! And what I said about Kim?''

''Analyze it yourself: 'more in love with yourself than anyone else, use people and discard them, good mind but doesn't exercise it.' Sound familiar, Suzanne?''

Suzanne sighed—deeply.

''Much too familiar. Much, much too familiar. It kills me to admit it, but that's me. Okay. Everything you've said so far is exactly correct. Now what do I do about it?''

''Well, now you start to be a human being.'' For example:

1. *Gold is found deep under the ground.* Sometimes the most interesting people don't go to discotheques. There are warm and worthwhile human beings all around you. They may not be tricked out in designer jeans or work in advertising agencies or be astronauts. They may be librarians or welders or insurance salesmen or bank tellers. But you can't measure the worth of an individual by the kind of work they do or the after-shave lotion or wristwatch or perfume they use.

2. *Look for the real qualities.* Cool talk, with-it expressions, and wisecracking are no substitute for genuine human warmth. Look for expressions of real feeling. The girl who makes dinner for you when you have the flu and the man who helps you move to your new apartment are worth more than all the pseudosophisticated plastic boys and girls who are in love with themselves. Remember the old Russian proverb ''It is action which is required— not words.'' Kim was all talk and no action. Instead of worrying about Suzanne's sexual needs, he popped ''poppers'' to intensify his own orgasm. Don't pay attention to what people *say*—pay attention to what they *do*—or *don't do*.

3. *Use yourself to set the example.* You will find people who are only as good or as bad as you are. Make yourself into a warm and loving person, and suddenly you will find warm and loving people swarming around you. Purge your

mind of all those empty soap-opera images of your ideal mate. Those electronic paper dolls don't exist and never existed. They are actors and actresses—nothing more and nothing less.

4. *Don't be afraid to feel*. A big part of Suzanne's problem was her hesitation to expose her own emotions to someone who didn't really feel anything. But she didn't have to worry because she had nothing to lose. If she really tried to plug her emotional energy into another person and he rejected her, it was his loss, not hers. And sooner or later she is bound to find someone that she can match up with—who will plug into her as perfectly as she plugs into him. That's what it's all about!

## 29
## Beyond Mental First-Aid

THE BEST WAY to deal with the suffering and unhappiness that come from life's worst problems is simply to *avoid* those problems. Does that sound too easy? Well, let's take a good hard look at it and see. As you walk along the street in wet weather, you see dozens of puddles in your path. You have two choices: You can go around them or you can splash through them. You'd think that everybody would naturally walk around a puddle. Who wants to get their feet wet, catch pneumonia, ruin a good pair of shoes, or soak their socks? Apparently a lot of people, because you see them sloshing through puddles right up to their ankles.

As you walk through life you find a lot of *emotional* puddles in your path; it's your decision whether to slosh through them or step around them. These emotional puddles have names like "drinking," "smoking," "drugs," "gambling," "living beyond your means," "cheating," and a whole bunch of other names like that. Plunk a foot into one of these puddles and you have an instant problem instead of an instant solution. And there's one other complication. When you step into one of these puddles you have no idea how deep it is. You can go in up to your ankles, up to your neck—or way over your head. Bill is a good example of that.

Bill was six feet tall, slim, with curly brown hair and an infectious grin. He looked about forty, maybe a little older. He wore a cream-colored broadcloth shirt with pearl buttons and well-fitted, dark gray-brown, cavalry-twill slacks. The top two buttons of his shirt were open to reveal something interesting around his neck. It was a thin gold chain holding up nine tiny block letters cut out of gold. They spelled *J-u-s-t L-u-c-k-y*.

"Does that mean what it says, Bill?"

He showed that grin.

"It sure does, Doc, but not the way that you might think."

"Want to tell me about it?"

"Sure—that's why I'm here! Let's see, I'm twenty-nine now—it was about a year ago that I bought that little trinket."

He paused and looked up.

"Surprised?"

"Uhm-hm. Double surprise. I'd assumed that someone gave it to you."

Bill paused expectantly.

"But you said 'double surprise,' Doctor. What's the other one?"

"I hope you don't mind but . . ."

"That I look five or ten years older than I really am?"

"Well, you said it. Might the two surprises be related?"

Bill chuckled.

"Can't fool you doctors, can we? Okay, here it is. Two years ago I was on top of the world. I ran a go-go stock brokerage house in Los Angeles. It was a small outfit with about seven salesmen, but we really rolled. We had a lot of musical people for clients—you know, rock groups, singers, musicians, arrangers. They made big money and they wanted good investments. We helped out. We did pretty well for a while."

"What do you call 'pretty well'?"

"I was making about three hundred fifty thousand dollars a year in commissions. I had a Lotus for weekdays and a Lamborghini for weekends. With all the trimmings, of course. The Lotus was black with white leather inside and a mother-of-pearl dashboard—nothing flashy. The Lamborghini was white—less formal—with black leather seats and trim. The dashboard was ebony and zebrawood. I had a little pad up above Franklin Canyon just outside Los Angeles. It had eleven bedrooms, ten bathrooms, and an orgy room. Well, that's what we called it. It was just a big room with a hot tub, a whirlpool spa, and about ten thousand dollars worth of ferns and tropical plants thrown around. A few orchids—not too many. And we did have a little waterfall—about eleven feet high. Helped keep the ferns moist."

Bill shook his head as he grinned.

"It all seems so crazy now that it's over."

"What do you mean 'over'?"

"I thought you'd have figured it all out by now, Doc."

"Maybe. But I'd rather hear it from you."

"Right. That was the fun part. What wasn't so funny was the rest of it. Cocaine, heroin, booze, marihuana, hash, and a couple of other things we smoked and sniffed that I still don't know what they were. And the chicks. We had the craziest collection of girls going through that place that you've ever seen in your life. We had a couple that loved to answer the door naked. You know, they'd be staying with us and the mailman would ring the bell to deliver a package and they'd race each other to the door stark naked just to see the look in the poor guy's face. Crazy."

Bill paused as if he were trying to remember something. Then he continued.

"So there I was. Twenty-seven years old, rich, living in Los Angeles, up to my neck in cars, dope, liquor, crazy broads. Working fourteen hours a day, staying up all night spaced out, and trying to get it all together to fight the stock market in the morning. Then the market started going down. I know, that's what it does. It goes up and it goes down. Well, it went fast and hard. And I was half out of my mind with drugs and the booze anyhow. I started taking tranquilizers just to make it until I got home. I started the morning with Valium, then switched to amphetamines. I had three martinis at lunch with some Acapulco Gold, a little coke in the afternoon when I'd start to run down. When I got home, it was French brandy and more Valium and then maybe some hash.''

Bill shook his head vigorously.

"I don't know! I was super crazy and getting crazier! I fell apart a couple of times, and they had to haul me off to de-toxify me. But it didn't really help. You see what it finally did to me? It put five—no, ten—years on my body. A twenty-nine-year-old boy with the body of a thirty-nine-year-old man. Weird, eh?''

Bill laughed.

"I knew I was going to sell my chips one day soon, and the only thing that kept me going was Joni. Joni was an airline stewardess who quit her job to be my secretary. Well, not really. I paid her five thousand dollars a month, but she was just living with me. She was the most beautiful person I ever met. I mean, she had a body that just wouldn't quit, and she really loved sex and . . . and . . . and what really mattered was she cared about me. I was a wild crazy hophead slowly losing my grip, and the only thing that kept me going was this beautiful little blonde saint. Oh, she was into drugs a little, but it was only for me.''

Bill thought a moment.

"Maybe it wasn't just for me. Anyhow, it was the twenty-third of December—I'll never forget the date. I'd just gotten back from an office party—it was two o'clock in the morning—and I was pretty well wired. I was in the hot tub trying to get my brain pulled free from too much hash. Joni was in the kitchen cooking. Well, not really cooking. You know, dope fiends do these insane little things. She was dissolving cocaine in ether. We were going to have a party the next night, and she had about a gallon of ether she was working with. I know it's weird, but that's what we do. After the cocaine is all dissolved, you soak marihuana in the ether and then dry it out. It gives you a bang that you just can't imagine. I don't know what it does to your mind, but dopers never worry about that until it's too late.''

Bill paused and looked blankly into space.

"Where was I?"

"Cooking the cocaine and ether?"

"Oh, yeah. Anyhow I was collapsed in the tub, and all I heard was this soft 'whoosh!' and a long loud terrible scream that I can still hear in my nightmares. I was out of that tub in one jump, and when I got to the kitchen I saw Joni there. The ether had exploded and she was burned—but bad. I went cold sober in about one second. I got the ambulance and all that."

Bill put his hand up to his mouth.

"Let me wait a minute, okay?"

"Sure, Bill."

After a few moments he went on.

"Anyhow, the last time I saw her was about three hours later in the intensive care unit. She was all wrapped in bandages—like a mummy. There were just these two bright little blue eyes peering out through little holes in her face bandage. I didn't know what to say—like an idiot. So I said, 'Gee, Joni, how'd something like that happen to you?' ''

It was obviously hard for Bill to continue but he went on.

"Do you know what she said, Doctor? She turned those pretty blue eyes up to me and whispered so I could hardly hear her: 'Just lucky, I guess. Just lucky.' Those were the last words she ever said. She died about an hour later.''

Bill fingered the letters around his neck.

"I went straight from the hospital to a jewelry store and had this made up—to remind me for the rest of my life what I lost—and *why*. Then I went home and poured about one hundred thousand dollars of really first-class dope down the toilet. Opium, cocaine, heroin, Pride of Jamaica, you name it. I broke every bottle of booze in the house. I took the pills and dumped them in the garbage disposal. That week I sold the cars and house and paid off all my debts. I closed the business and spent the next two months just thinking."

"What did you think about, Bill?"

"I thought, Doctor, about how close I came to being 'Just Lucky' like Joni. I was getting myself into every kind of trouble there was. I should have been happy—after all I supposedly had everything. But actually I had *nothing*. And I was really lucky. A few months later they had a big investigation of my ex-company, and two of my former partners went up the river—five years each in the federal pen. I was an expert in messing up my life and I figured the only way out for me was to go straight. So, I went straight. Straighter than the straightest arrow you've ever seen. I don't drink. I don't smoke. I won't even take an aspirin. I don't mess around with crazies anymore. Now I work for a big brokerage firm. I sell a lot, I make a good living, and that's enough for me. I put in my eight hours, and the rest of my life is my own. I do a lot of biking, and I built a little sailboat last fall with my fiancée. She's as straight as I am. I'm never going to see her blown away like I saw . . . well, there's no point starting with that again. I don't know, but I think I've discovered the secret of happiness, Doctor. At least for me. If you want to feel *good*, you have to act *good*. There's no such thing as a free lunch."

Bill is right. The only way to avoid life's worst problems is to *avoid* them. I know it goes against all the popular wisdom, but it's the only way. If you don't ever want to risk becoming an alcoholic, don't drink. It's that simple. Instead of enmeshing yourself in all those wonderful explanations like "You have to learn how to drink" and "Alcohol relaxes me" and all the rest, you just have to eliminate one of the big puddles from the pathway of your life. The same principle holds true for smoking. Cigarette smoking causes lung cancer. That's all there is to it. If you don't smoke, you won't get lung cancer—except for very rare forms of the disease that may affect nonsmokers. As of today over 20 percent of all cancer deaths in the United States are from lung cancer—from cigarettes—with the figure increasing every year. If you don't ever want to have to face the monster of lung cancer, just don't smoke. Is it easy? It's almost too easy. That's why so few people do it.

You can't afford to throw money away? (Who can?) Then don't gamble. The financial loss and suffering and tragedy that come from gambling can be avoided by *not* gambling. Is that oversimplifying things? Maybe. Let's simplify it even more. If you don't want to lose, don't gamble. If you don't want to get poison ivy, don't go where poison ivy is. But you knew that already, didn't you?

Back in the 1880s Joel Chandler Harris published an interesting book of children's stories called *Uncle Remus, His Son's and His Sayings*. The most interesting story of all is about a little rabbit known as Brer Rabbit and something known as the Tar Baby. The Tar Baby was a great big doll made of sticky tar and set up by the side of the road on a warm summer day. Brer Rabbit was strolling down the road and found the Tar Baby. Although he knew better he couldn't resist the temptation to touch him. He reached out gingerly to probe the Tar Baby—first with one little paw—which immediately became stuck to the Tar Baby's tarry exterior. He immediately tried to free himself by pushing off with the other paw—which also got stuck.

You can imagine the rest. In spite of all his struggling Brer Rabbit became trapped by the Tar Baby.

*The world you live in is filled with Tar Babies!* Drinking, smoking, taking drugs, gambling, living beyond your means, using sex to get yourself in trouble, overeating, and fifty other problems are all Tar Babies. Once you get started with them, each time you try to free yourself, you run the risk of getting stuck tighter and tighter. The next time you stroll down the street and see a Tar Baby, run, do not walk, the other way. Ginnie knows what *that* means.

Ginnie was tall, olive-skinned, and looked as if she had just stepped out of an Italian travel poster. Her dark eyes flashed as she spoke. "Would you believe it, Doctor, I was once Miss Rome!"

"You lived in Italy?"

"Italy? Who said 'Italy'? I was talking about Rome, New York. But seriously, that's the way it all started. I'm from a nice Italian family. My father is a doctor—he's a professor of surgery and has his own practice besides—and my mother taught history before she got married. I don't know how I got into that beauty contest business, but I guess I caught the bug when I was in high school. I was Miss Apple Blossom in my senior year."

Ginnie laughed.

"It all seemed like fun then but—what was that story you told me about last time? You know the rabbit and how he got stuck?"

"The Tar Baby?"

"Yes, that's it! Well, I'm the original Italian Tar Baby. I mean, it was just identical. Look, after I graduated high school I went to work as a receptionist in an advertising agency. I was going to college part time studying acting. I had all these tremendous fantasies in those days. You know, I thought I was going to be a movie star or something. I don't really know *what* I was thinking. Then I got the chance to do some cigarette commercials—local stuff, nothing big. But I was a dummy, and I got the idea that it was 'sophisticated' to smoke. So I became a smoker. Then my boss started taking me around just to be there when he entertained his customers. Nothing out of line, but at least once a week I was eating out at fancy restaurants and going to night clubs. Well, you know what happened, don't you?''

Without waiting for an answer, Ginnie went on.

''I started drinking. Not too much. Maybe a martini or two every evening we went out. And then a little more. Now maybe that doesn't mean much to you, but a girl from a good Italian family sitting around in a bar smoking and drinking was a little out of line. Of course I started fighting with my family, and I finally had to move to an apartment. That's when—what did you call it—the Tar Baby really took over. You see, I was all alone in this little apartment, and I was used to living in this big house with four brothers and sisters and a couple aunts and my parents. So I went crazy for company. But not for long.''

''What do you mean, 'not for long'?''

Ginnie started to reach into her purse, then changed her mind.

''I was going to look for a cigarette, but I'm not smoking anymore. Anyhow, after a while, I wasn't crazy for company, I was just crazy. I started going out every night just so I wasn't alone. I went with weird people—you know, you never knew what they did for a living and most of the time you didn't want to know. I started modeling, and then it was more beauty contests. I finally met this actors' agent and we got married.''

''How long were you married?''

Ginnie pursed her lips.

''Four months. Long enough to get pregnant but not long enough to have a baby.''

''What do you mean, 'not long enough to have a baby'?''

Ginnie's dark eyes suddenly filled with tears.

''Look, I was twenty-two, in trouble with my family, drinking, running around with weirdos, married to a Swede for four months and then divorced, *and* pregnant. What else could I do?''

"Did you really have to have the abortion?"

Ginnie went pale.

"No, looking back on it, probably not. But remember what was happening. to me. Every time I tried to rescue myself, I went in deeper. If it hadn't been for the 'misunderstanding,' I don't know where I'd be now. No, that's not true. I know where I'd be. I'd be wearing a cheap housedress with a number stenciled over the left breast pocket. I'd be in jail. When I think back on it, it makes me shake all over. I almost got myself into jail!''

"What happened?"

"Well, I was feeling really down in the dumps one night. It was about three weeks after my abortion, and I was all alone in my little apartment when one of my boyfriends called up and asked if I wanted to go for a ride. At that moment I would have gone for a ride with the Hunchback of Notre Dame. So he came by and picked me up in this new Mercedes 450. We just cruised around for a couple of hours. He stopped in once at some all night grocery to buy dog food. He has this big Doberman that ate constantly, and he put the bags in the trunk. That was the 'misunderstanding.' He was just taking me home when he went through a yellow light—but barely. We heard this siren and a police car pulled in front of us. Then two more unmarked cars suddenly appeared. I didn't like the way it looked. I said to myself: 'Oh, Ginnie, you're getting in deeper and deeper. Now what's going to happen?' If it happened now I'd say it differently.''

"What would you say?"

"I'd say, 'Tar Baby, here I come!' You see, Frank had gone through the yellow light, so technically that gave them the right to search the car. That's what they'd been looking for. Looking back on it, they'd been following us all the time just waiting for the chance to grab us. Do you know what they found in the trunk?''

"No, but I'll bet it wasn't dog food."

"Smart doctor. It was a mere fifteen pounds of cocaine. Imagine that idiot, driving around for an hour with fifteen pounds of cocaine in his trunk! And the police right behind him all the time! Well, I spent about six hours in jail— with a fascinating group of girls. Prostitutes, alcoholics, drug addicts, child beaters, petty thieves—really the world's losers. But there was one scary thing that they all had in common."

"What was that, Ginnie?"

"They all played the Tar Baby game. When they first got in trouble, instead of pulling away once and for all, they went back for more. One of the girls in there for hustling was a girl I knew from high school. I mean, it could have been me! Well, I managed to call my dad, and he came down in about six minutes flat. He had me out of there in no time, and he convinced the police that I didn't have anything to do with the dope, that I was just a dummy—which I was. He closed up my apartment and moved me back home the next day. I'm back in college now and I think I want to be a history teacher like mom. In a couple of months I'm going to be engaged, and this time it's to a nice Italian boy. It may sound funny, but I feel more comfortable with him. You know, we understood each other right from the start."

The suffering and unhappiness that Bill and Ginnie went through really go far beyond their individual situations. They touch a far more basic problem—the problem of *lifestyle*. One hundred years ago the pattern of life in the United States, Europe and Latin America was relatively simple. People sacrificed to get the best possible education. Then they struggled to get a good secure job. Their next goal was to marry someone decent and hardworking and raise a family. Husband, wife and children all lived and worked together, and finally the children married and had children and the cycle began again. For the most part parents and grown-up children lived in the same city if not the same neighborhood. They were constantly in touch with each other and usually worked in the same business or at least the same general type of area. If any of them had a problem, they could immediately count on all the resources of their family to help them. Money, influence, advice, reassurance—it was all available in relative abundance.

Marriage was a lot easier. Most people married within their ethnic and social groups. You knew whom you were marrying because your parents knew their parents or they knew somebody who knew their parents. You knew what to expect from your husband or wife—your roles were already created. If your parents were Greek, you knew what was expected of you in marriage—and you knew what your husband or wife expected. If your parents were Norwegian, you knew what the Norwegian culture set up as the norms within a marriage. If you married someone from your own background, you had an excellent chance of a happy and stable marriage.

But then things gradually began to change. Subtly at first and then not so subtly, the current of materialism began to erode the traditional patterns of human existence. The single most important goal in life became *getting*. You had to *get* an important job. You had to *get* a prestigious education (not necessarily a *good* education). You had to *get* a beautiful wife. And people really *got*. They got cars and they got stereos and they got color TVs and they got motor homes and they got videotape recorders and they got diamond rings and they got fur coats and they got jobs with impressive titles and they got elegant wardrobes and they got inflated ideas of their own importance. They also got ulcers and depression and divorce and abortions and VD and drug addiction and alcoholism like never before in the history of the world. In the bargain they got fifty more of the world's worst problems—problems that used to affect people only in novels or in movies.

By the way if you don't remember, ask your parents—or

even your grandparents—how many of their friends smoked marihuana. Ask them how many of their acquaintances were divorced. Ask them how many of their friends had abortions. Ask them if they knew *anyone* who had been arrested by the police. Then ask yourself how many people *you* know in those four categories. That gives you some idea of how society has deteriorated in the past five decades or so.

There's one terribly destructive effect of this relatively new illusion of *getting*. It's the *attempt* to substitute material values for human values. I will never forget that very wealthy patient of mine who once said—in all seriousness—"If you have an excellent videotape recorder and a really great stereo, you don't need any friends."

But that's the basic problem. To acquire material things you have to work. But since the list of material things is endless, your work has to be endless as well. You are then condemned to spend most of your waking hours trying to make a lot of money. Then you can pay for things you don't really need so you can distract yourself in the few hours of tension-filled leisure you manage to steal from your tension-filled work. Of course, you don't have time for such luxuries as friends and family, and in those thousands of hours you spend watching television and movies and video cassettes you see only people who are desperately running after material things in an attempt to *buy* the happiness that is never for sale.

Let's take a long hard look at modern life. Most children grow up in homes in which their parents are working so hard to support their illusions of *getting* material things that they don't have time to educate their children. That means "educate" in the true sense of the word. It's not really so important if the kids know that Gaborone is the capital of the African nation of Botswana. They can always look it up when the time comes. But it is vital for the parents to teach their kids about what alcohol does to them and about how cigarettes will give them cancer. Most parents don't do that! It's just as vital for the parents to educate their children about sex and about venereal disease. They don't do that either. That's left to the schools—to strangers who have hardly any interest in your children. What the kids *do* learn at school is how to roll a joint of marihuana, where to go for an abortion, and all the other little skills of modern life.

The other thing that most parents forget to teach their children is what human existence is all about. They forget to teach them that murdering other people is bad—even if you call it a "war." They forget to teach them that kindness and consideration for other people make your life better. They forget to teach them that education and study are keys to becoming a better person. They forget to show them by example the benefits of honesty and fairness.

When those kids get old enough they get away from their parents as fast as they can. "Going away to college" is the usual technique. Then it's a job in a distant city. If the parents live in Dallas, New York is the place that calls. If Mom and Dad live in New York, then it's off to San Francisco. Once they arrive in a strange city among strangers, things move pretty fast. Like Ginnie, they feel isolated and alone. That's the kind of loneliness that breeds empty friendships, drugs, alcohol, hasty marriages, and even hastier divorces. The parents suffer, the children suffer, and the only one who benefits is the telephone company on Christmas Day, when lonely and isolated people exchange platitudes over long-distance wires.

Is that picture too gloomy? I don't think so. Check around and you'll find it's right on target. The index of personal unhappiness is increasing year by year. Just compare the statistics. Every year there are more divorces, more abortions, more suicides, more alcoholism, more drug addiction, and more cases of depression. What's the answer? Well, it's staring us right in the face. If we open our eyes, we can see it, and if we open our minds, we can apply it.

There are actually two major lifestyles in the world today. The *traditional* and the so-called *modern*. (I say "so-called *modern*" because there is really nothing modern about it, but we'll see about that in a moment.) We are now trapped in the *"modern"* lifestyle, which is based on the following principles:

1. Happiness comes from money and what money buys—nothing else.
2. Self-destructive behavior like drug addiction, alcoholism, paranoia, sexual perversions, stealing, and the rest are all justified by some vague something called "freedom of choice."
3. There are no standards of behavior or values in life except the impulse of the moment.
4. Emotional ties like love between husband and wife and parents and children are obstacles to "freedom."
5. Marriage has no meaning.
6. Life has no meaning.

The *traditional* lifestyle looks at things differently:

1. Happiness comes from warm and loving personal relationships.
2. Self-destructive behavior doesn't make sense, and people who are self-destructive should be avoided.
3. The standards of behavior are honesty, fairness, decency, and, above all, humanity.
4. The key ingredient for personal happiness is *love*—love between parents and children, love between husband and wife.
5. A happy loving marriage is the nucleus of personal fulfillment.
6. The meaning of life is to shower love upon those who love you, to make this world a better place because you have lived in it.

The choice is yours—a *"modern"* life or a *traditional* life. By the way, "modern" comes from the same root as the word "mode," and it means "fashionable." Does that ring a bell? Think carefully. Whenever you read or hear the word "modern," it's almost always because *someone is trying to sell you something.* *"Modern"* means "buy," "acquire," "spend." "Modern" means you pay twice as much for a new model that lasts half as long. Sound familiar?

We all know the familiar saying about money: "Income: one thousand dollars. Expenses: nine hundred ninety-nine dollars. Result: *happiness.* Income: one thousand dollars. Expenses: one thousand and one dollars. Result: *misery.*"

Well, that's exactly the way it is in dealing with life's worst problems. If your common sense and intelligence add up to just a fraction more than your problems, the final result will be happiness. But if your problems are always one step ahead of you, the outcome will be misery. That's a permanent fact of life that you might as well face— because you can't avoid it.

There's one more fact of life that is unavoidable: Your happiness does not drop out of a tree into your backyard. It is the direct result of your own personal choices. *If you want to feel good, you have to act good.* The way your life turns out is a direct result of the thousand choices you make every day. Each and every one of life's worst problems that we have dealt with up to now can be avoided by making the right choice. Now you know what the choices are and you know what the consequences are. The rest is up to you!